Mother Teresa

To Live, To Love, To Witness

Lush Gjergji

Mother Teresa
To Live, To Love, To Witness

Her Spiritual Way

Translated by Jordan Aumann, O.P.

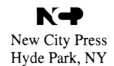

New City Press
Hyde Park, NY

Published in the United States by New City Press
202 Cardinal Rd., Hyde Park, NY 12538
©1998 New City Press

First Published as *Vivere, Amare, Testimoniare—La Spiritualità di Madre Teresa*
by Editrice Velar, Bergamo, Italy
©1995 Editrice Velar

Translated by Jordan Aumann, O.P.

Cover designed by Nick Cianfarani

Library of Congress Cataloging-in-Publication Data:
Gjergji, Lush.
    [Amare, vivere, testimoniare. English]
    Mother Teresa : to live, to love, to witness : her spiritual way /
Lush Gjergji.
       p. cm.
    ISBN 1-56548-109-7
    1. Spiritual life—Catholic Church. 2. Catholic Church—
Doctrines. 3. Teresa, Mother, 1910- I. Title.
    BX2350.2.G5913 1998
    248.4'82—dc21   97-47483

Printed in Taiwan

Contents

Foreword

The book which you are about to read originated from a careful reflection on two of the basic themes of the Christian faith: to live with Christ and to bear witness with the Church. It was written by constantly drawing upon biblical sources, the teaching of the Church, the documents of the Second Vatican Council, and the precious testimony of the faith and thought of Mother Teresa. Father Lush Gjergji has carefully examined the work of the Holy Spirit and then adapted it to his own thought and feelings so that it could be expressed in human language and thus touch our hearts directly.

To live and to love

Many thinkers have attempted to describe the true essence of life; others have sought to discover its meaning; still others have shunned the question entirely. One alone has been able to say of himself: "I am the life" (Jn 11:25). Christ not only *is* the life, he also is the one who "gives it in abundance." Consequently, we receive our life as a gift, and the best way to give it its fullest meaning is to live for others. Christ himself gave us this teaching when he said: "Unless the grain of wheat falls to the earth and dies, it remains just a grain of wheat" (Jn 11:24). So the mystery of life also includes death, and the ancient wise men taught that "whatever one would not die for, vanishes forever." From this it follows that love alone can serve as the authentic basis of life.

The true meaning of life is to be found in a life governed by love. The worst thing possible is not to have life at all, but any life that lacks love is still a deficient life. One thing is absolutely certain: God loves us. We are beings that are loved. We are loved even more because we have been created by Love in order to love. If we want to live love, to learn how to love, we must learn how to die to ourselves. Love vanishes at the point that it fails to give of itself. Therefore, in order to live one's life in accordance with the eternal value of love, it is necessary to know how to give, even to the point of risking one's life. This is the most authentic type of witness.

To witness

To bear witness means to put into practice the Word of God every day of our life. If we really let ourselves be infused with divine life, if we are inflamed with divine love, then we shall be able to bear witness, to shine forth and illumine. A lamp does not have to be preceded by other lesser degrees of light; it is in itself an authentic source of light. Similarly, a life lived with love is a testimony that resounds in the hearts of people even when they seem to be far from experiencing it. We may have forgotten many words in our life, but the word of a love that illumines us will remain with us for all eternity. In order to speak to us in the course of history, the Lord has made use of many people. In the end, he has spoken to us through his Son, who has gathered together in his Mystical Body all those who have been enlightened by the grace of the cross and the power of his resurrection. Accordingly, through the Church he speaks to them of the love that emanates from a life of goodness.

With thoughts such as these, Father Lush Gjergji brings us close to that life of love that is also manifested in the face of Mother Teresa. I hope that this book will enkindle in all of you who read it a spark that will ignite that same love in your daily life. May the life of each one of us become an open book whose pages are stamped with love and witness, praising God for the marvelous examples that he gives us. And may Mary, the highly favored daughter of the Church, be a model for the living Church which we all are.

Vinko Cardinal Puljic'
Archbishop of Sarajevo, Bosnia-Herzegovina

Abbreviations

AA   *Apostolicam Actuositatem* (Decree on the Apostolate of Lay People)

AG   *Ad Gentes Divinitus* (Decree on the Church's Missionary Activity)

CCC   *Catechism of the Catholic Church*

DV   *Dei Verbum* (Dogmatic Constitution on Divine Revelation)

GS   *Gaudium et Spes* (Constitution on the Church in the Modern World)

IM   *Inter Mirifica* (Decree on the Means of Social Communication)

LG   *Lumen Gentium* (Dogmatic Constitution on the Church)

MC   *Marialis Cultus* (Apostolic Exhortation on Devotion to Mary)

MD   *Magnam Dei Matris* (Encyclical on the Rosary)

MS   *Misericordiam Suam* (Introduction to the New Order of Penance)

NA   *Nostra Aetate* (Declaration on the Relations of the Church to Non-Christian Religions)

PC   *Perfectae Caritatis* (Decree on the Up-to-Date Renewal of Religious Life)

PO   *Presbyterorum Ordinis* (Decree on the Ministry and Life of Priests)

RM   *Redemptoris Mater* (Encyclical on the Mother of the Redeemer)

SC   *Sacrosanctum Concilium* (Constitution on the Sacred Liturgy)

UR   *Unitatis Redintegratio* (Decree on Ecumenism)

Note: All quotations from the documents of the Second Vatican Council are taken from *Vatican Council II: The Conciliar and Post Conciliar Documents*, edited by Austin Flannery, O.P., Liturgical Press, Collegeville, MN, 1975.

To Live
and to Love

Centuries of Waiting

In times past,
God spoke in fragmentary and varied ways
to our fathers through the prophets;
in this, the final age,
he has spoken to us through his Son,
whom he has made heir of all things
and through whom
he first created the universe.
Hebrews 1:1-2

God has created us for great things:
to love and to give love.
Mother Teresa

All of human history is nothing other than a continuous interweaving of past, present and future, alternating between expectation and realization, anticipation and fulfillment. To hope for a better future is common to every human being.

Waiting is a part of life. In fact, all life is a continuous waiting period which begins even before birth. The infant that is to be born, what will it be like? Will it be more like its father or its mother? Will it be a boy or a girl? Then, when the child is born, we await its first smile, its first word, its first steps. And the expectant waiting continues throughout the period of infancy, the school years, puberty and adolescence, maturity, raising such questions as the choice of work, family, health, wealth, success, happiness.

The sick person awaits a cure; the poor person, money; the prisoner, freedom; the unemployed, work. I also am waiting for something or someone, as others wait for something from me. Whether or not this waiting is fulfilled depends on many persons and a variety of circumstances.

The world and the entire human race have waited for centuries for things without knowing what they were waiting for: electricity, the telephone, radio, television, the airplane, in a word, all kinds of scientific, technological and industrial progress. The same thing is true in the field of medicine; for example the discovery of penicillin in modern times, and now the world awaits victory in the battle against cancer and AIDS.

Humanity continues to wait—for a life that is more equitable; for peace and justice for all; for a world in which through love we shall relate to every human being as our neighbor, our brother or sister.

Only in the area of religion can we say that, although life is a continual vigil, it is also a fulfillment, at least in part, of our expectations. The Second Vatican Council has expressed this concept very well: "The joy and hope, the grief and anguish of . . . our time, especially of those who are poor or afflicted in any way, are the joy and hope, the grief and anguish of the followers of Christ as well. Nothing that is genuinely human fails to find an echo in their hearts" (GS 1).

The one awaited throughout the centuries is Jesus Christ, the Savior of the world, in whom "the mystery of man truly becomes clear" (GS 22). "Christ is the head and exemplar of that renewed humanity, imbued with that brotherly love, sincerity and spirit of peace, to which all men aspire. . . . So it is not without reason that Christ is hailed by the faithful as 'the hope of the nations and their Savior'" (AG 8).

He is truth made flesh, man, love, salvation, good news, and hence the only possibility for radically changing human history.

Jesus has come to reveal the Father. In the Old Testament God was known as the God of fear, of anger and of punishment. The coming of Jesus completely changed that concept. In Jesus, God is love and pardon. (Mother Teresa)

For the Christian, who with faith and love has accepted Jesus Christ as the Father's revelation, the waiting is over. Jesus is God with us, in our midst and for us. After the coming of Christ, and especially after his death and resurrection, life has a meaning that is more profound, more beautiful and more certain, because in Jesus Christ everything has been renewed, changed and perfected.

In Jesus Christ we accept and live this liberating good news: God is with us through his great love and pardon. He continuously comes to us; he is present in our history, not simply as a visitor, but as the God-Man who loves us and offers his life for our salvation. In so doing, he becomes the new Adam, the perfect man, the one authentic exemplar for humanity.

Because of his coming, we can await complete freedom: from the slavery of sin, evil and death itself. In Jesus we can become new persons, children of God, capable of living in peace and harmony with ourselves, with others and with God. Because God has become a man like us in all things except sin (cf. Heb 4:15).

This kind of talk may today seem superfluous or even ingenuous. We are already truly free, capable of being ourselves, of living and making responsible decisions for ourselves and for others. We don't need any help from outside, not even from God! Once again we find ourselves face to face with the pride that prompted Adam and Eve, and then the whole human race, to say no to God and yes to evil.

The predominant influence of science, technology and progress is more evident today than ever before. But it can in no way resolve the fundamental problems of human existence: the meaning of human nature and activity; questions concerning justice, love, happiness, and human relationships within the family and in society at large, on the national and international level. For these answers it is necessary to turn to Jesus Christ, who is "the Alpha and the Omega, the first and the last, the beginning and the end" (Rv 22:13). Only then will the absurd rivalry between us and God and among ourselves come to an end.

Jesus comes to us in three different ways:

— By being born of the Virgin Mary, God becomes man;

— He continuously comes to us and is in our midst through the Church and the sacramental life of the eucharist;

— "He will come again in glory to judge the living and the dead, and his kingdom will have no end," as we say in the Nicene Creed (CCC, p. 49).

We constantly live with great and small expectations. Sometimes we succeed and sometimes we fail. But this is the way we experience the dynamism and the drama of life, of the future as yet unknown and beyond our control. And precisely because of this fascinating aspect, life is at once beautiful and perilous.

The authentic expectation for us Christians has been revealed and given to us in Jesus Christ, who is the way, the truth and the life. "In him, in whom God reconciled all things to himself, men find the fullness of their religious life" (NA 2).

The dynamism between expectation and attainment corresponds to hope and to faith. One cannot believe and love and at the same time fail to hope and to act on that hope. We can only be creative through faith and love by responsibly collaborating with God, who is constantly creative and active. Mother Teresa puts it this way:

All of us, you and I, should use what God has given us, that for which God created us. For God has created us for great things: to love and to give love. . . . That is why we are able to give Jesus to others. . . . People do not hunger for us, for our works, for our care. People hunger for God, for Jesus Christ, for the eucharist. . . . This is love in action or active love. While on earth, we cannot see Jesus and therefore cannot even express our love for him. But every day we see and live through our love. Every day we see and live with our neighbor, and therefore we can and should do what we would do for Christ if he were visible. We should be available for God so he can use us. Let us put love into practice, and then the hopes of the world will not be in vain, futile or frustrated, because through love we find LOVE, *Jesus Christ.*

Then, speaking of the hopes of the poor, Mother Teresa once told me:

Money is not enough. . . . My poor need to be loved with the heart and served with our hands. Christ uses me and all of us so as to put us in contact with the poor. Wherever I go I see one thing: People have such a great need of God. Therefore we should help them to seek him and find him. . . . The Advent season is like the springtime in nature, when everything is renewed and is fresh and luxuriant. The season of Advent should fulfill in us this expectation: to make Jesus incarnate and living in us.

God Becomes Human

The birth of every baby is a great miracle of nature, of the parents' love, of a life that begins in us and gives rise to great expectations. Every baby makes us more human, more good, more tender. It gives us new breath, as it were; breath that is cleaner and deeper, because it represents the springtime of life. Meditating on new life, Tagore said: "As long as God makes the flowers bloom and babies be born, humanity will have a future."

This is true for every new birth on earth. But how much more does it apply to the birth of the infant Jesus, which was awaited not only by his parents, Mary and Joseph, not only by a town and nation, Bethlehem and Israel, and not only at a particular time, but by the whole human race. In him every human being is born and reborn.

The birth of Jesus is for us a font of inexhaustible joy, of hope, of life and of love, because it represents an embrace between heaven and earth.

Luke the evangelist describes this extraordinary event and fills in some of the details for us:

— The birth of Jesus was foretold by the angel Gabriel, who said to Mary: "Rejoice, O highly favored daughter! The Lord is with you. Blessed are you among women. . . . You shall conceive and bear a son and give him the name Jesus" (Lk 1:28-31).

— This infant is not like any other. "Great will be his dignity and he will be called Son of the Most High . . . and his reign will be without end" (Lk 1:32-33).

— The birth of Jesus is not the usual, natural birth, the fruit of parental love. It is the fruit of the action of the Holy Spirit, who will "come upon you, and the power of the Most High will overshadow you; hence, the holy offspring to be born will be called Son of God" (Lk 1:35-36).

— Jesus was not born in a family home, as was customary at the time. While Joseph and Mary were at Bethlehem to register, "the days of her confinement were completed. She gave birth to her first-born son and wrapped him in swaddling clothes and laid him in a manger, because there was no room for them in the place where travelers lodged" (Lk 2:6-7).

Meditating on the birth of Jesus, Mother Teresa said:

We thank God that he gave his Son Jesus to be born into the world as we are and to be like us in all things except sin. In becoming man, God has manifested the grandeur and beauty of human life. . . . He wants to give himself to us in our hearts, together with joy and peace. And his coming can bring to each one of you that peace and that joy that he wants to give you. Let us pray earnestly that we may obtain this grace for our hearts, for our community, for the Church and for the whole world.

The angels were the first to rejoice at the birth of Jesus and then to announce peace and joy to the shepherds, praising the Lord and proclaiming to humankind: "Glory to God in high heaven, peace on earth to those on whom his favor rests" (Lk 2:12).

The coming of Jesus is the manifestation of God's love for humankind, and from this love is born true peace.

Let us pray that we may be able to welcome Jesus at Christmas, not in the cold manger of our heart, but with a heart full of love and humility, a heart warm with reciprocal love like that of Mary. (Mother Teresa)

To live the Christmas message today means to open our hearts to Jesus-Love, to acknowledge him and make him incarnate in our daily life. Mother Teresa lived the Christmas theme constantly. It prompted her to love, to act and to serve under the inspiration and motion of the Holy Spirit. The witness of her living faith invites us also to live this love of God and of neighbor.

Every time we let Jesus love others through us, it is Christmas. (Mother Teresa)

Eight days after his birth, Jesus was circumcised and "the name Jesus was given the child, the name the angel had given him before he was conceived" (Lk 2:21).

Simeon, a just and pious man, was awaiting the redemption of Israel, and the Holy Spirit was upon him. Inspired by the Spirit, he came to the temple, and when the parents brought in the child Jesus for the customary ritual prescribed by the law, Simeon took the child in his arms and blessed God, saying: "Now, Master, you can dismiss your servant in peace; you have fulfilled your word. For my eyes have witnessed your saving deed displayed for all the peoples to see: a revealing light to the Gentiles, the glory of your people Israel" (Lk 2:29-32). Simeon had recognized the child and he gave testimony, pointing him out to others as the light that illumines the nations, that is, all the peoples on the earth. The prophetess Anna did the same thing (cf. Lk 2:36-38).

To indicate the universality of the salvation brought by Jesus, the gospel also tells us about the three Magi, who came to Jerusalem from the east and then went on to Bethlehem to look for the newborn king. "We observed his star at its rising and have come to pay him homage" (Mt 2:1-12).

"The child's father and mother were marveling at what was being said about him" (Lk 2:33). Mother Teresa, however, used these incidents of the gospel to comment as follows:

The humility of Jesus is manifested in the manger, in the flight into Egypt, in his hidden life at Nazareth, in the eucharist . . . in submitting to the hatred of his persecutors, in the terrible suffering of his passion and death.

The coming of Jesus at Bethlehem brought joy to the world and to every human heart. The same Jesus continues to come into our hearts in holy communion. He wants to give us the same joy, the same peace. . . .

After a long and silent adoration of the eucharist Mother Teresa said:

I cannot imagine a day without Jesus, because he is my life, my love; he is everything to me. He came to give us the good news that God loves us, that God is love, that he loves you and me, and that we should love one another as he loves each one of us. . . . When we look at the manger, we understand how much he loves us through his suffering. When

we contemplate the cross, we understand how much he loved us: He died on the cross because he loved us, and he wants us to love one another as he loved us.

God's love for us is therefore intimately linked to suffering. The same thing can be said about our love for God and neighbor.

Christ came among us to place charity in its proper perspective. Everything was beautiful in heaven; so what was it that attracted Jesus to earth? The Son of God wanted to demonstrate what it means to be man, to remain in the womb for nine months, completely dependent on his mother. That is why we say: Rich though he was, he became poor and defenseless. (Mother Teresa)

The birth of Jesus illustrates especially God's love for humanity. The humility, poverty and suffering of Jesus are proof of that love and necessary elements of our life. I once asked Mother Teresa: "How can you be so humble when you are so loved and highly esteemed throughout the world?" She answered:

Humility is the most secure path to sanctity, because God can then do great things with us, as he did with Mary. Jesus teaches us: Learn of me, for I am humble. . . . It is necessary to have a heart that is humble and pure and to accept God's will; then everything is easy.

The Second Vatican Council has stated: "All . . . are called to this union with Christ, who is the light of the world, from whom we go forth, through whom we live, and toward whom our whole life is directed" (LG 3).

At Bethlehem everyone was filled with joy: the shepherds, the angels, the Magi, Joseph and Mary. Joy was also the distinctive characteristic of the first Christians. During the persecutions their faces were radiant with joy. . . . The entire life of Paul can be summed up in one phrase: "I belong to Jesus." Nothing can separate me from the love of Christ; neither suffering nor persecution nor anything at all. . . . That is why Paul was filled with joy. We too should always be filled with joy, and we should carry this joy and the love of God to others. (Mother Teresa)

Prepare the Way of the Lord

Reform your lives!
The reign of God is at hand. . . .
A herald's voice in the desert:
Prepare the way of the Lord,
make straight his paths.
Matthew 4:2-3

The most beautiful thing about Mary
is that when Jesus entered her life,
she immediately went in haste
to the house of Elizabeth
in order to give Jesus to her and her son.
Mother Teresa

Our life is full of personal contacts, conversations and encounters of various kinds. Today there have been such great advances in the means of communication that the world is becoming smaller and smaller. At the same time interpersonal relationships are becoming more rare, strained and anonymous. We speak, work and live always in great haste, on the run. As a result we lose the joy of meeting a human person that speaks, smiles, lives and loves. Our conversation is directed over our shoulder as we hasten on our way.

What does it mean today to communicate? First of all, it means to be sincere, cordial and open; to think, speak and act coherently. Instead, for many people the use of words has become a means of concealing and defending oneself and for deceiving or attacking one's neighbor, rather than a means of communication that truly expresses one's thoughts and feelings.

To communicate means to let others be themselves, to make progress by enriching ourselves through contact with others, thus cultivating a profound sense of community and fellowship.

Christians are constantly called upon to communicate with themselves, with others and with God. They are also called upon to communicate

God to others, to prepare the way of the Lord, as was done by John the Baptist, in imitation of Mary.

Our Lady set out in haste for the hill country and stayed there for three months in order to do the work of a servant for her aged cousin Elizabeth. . . . We have to possess before we can give. One who has the mission of giving to others must first grow in the knowledge of God and his love. . . . Mary's care for others was so great that she made Nazareth a refuge for God. Use your tongue for the good of others; out of the abundance of the heart, the mouth speaks. (Mother Teresa)

Our union with God is not only a personal gesture; it is a witness, a sign of his presence in our midst.

After adoration in the chapel in order to know, love and serve God, we go forth to find and love the same Jesus whom we have adored in the eucharist; to give witness to our faith by our love and service. (Mother Teresa)

It is not possible to experience God as love and not daily bear witness to him for others. Every apostolic mission for others springs from this, making us channels of a life infused by God.

After various national and international awards, and especially after receiving the Nobel Peace Prize in 1979, Mother Teresa said to me:

Now I am going to Rome to spend a few days with our Sisters. Then I shall meet the Holy Father. I have decided to withdraw from public life and also from the government of our Congregation. I shall go back to the village of the lepers.

And that is what she set out to do. But John Paul II could not accept such a great loss to the Church. So he said to her: "Mother, you are an authentic witness to Christ and the gospel. Therefore you should go wherever we send you to bear witness to all of God's love."

When I met her some months later, I asked her: "How is it that you are still active?" She answered with a smile:

The Holy Father told me that I must continue working, visiting our houses and bearing witness to Jesus throughout the world. So I am doing what he asked of me, that is, I am doing God's will.

The Holy Father visited India in 1986. Several times he and Mother Teresa walked together through the streets of misery. He visited the lepers, the house of the dying and other centers conducted by the Missionaries of Charity in Calcutta. It was a lengthy and arduous pastoral visit in a land of suffering and contradictions.

When the Pope returned to Rome, a journalist asked him: "Your Holiness, this was a long journey, and I would suppose that it was also very exhausting. How did you experience the reality of India?"

The Holy Father replied: "It was not a difficult journey. Rather, it was a very easy apostolic journey, because I had Mother Teresa at my side. When I preached to the people about Christianity and about love, it was enough to point to Mother Teresa and tell them: Mother Teresa is Christianity. The people immediately understood."

For her part, Mother Teresa said:

The eucharist is the font of Christian life. The eucharist is incomplete if it does not lead you to love and service of the poor.

The most beautiful example of how we should accept, love and bear witness to Jesus is Our Lady, and especially in her visit to Elizabeth:

Mary was a true missionary, because she was not afraid to be the handmaid of the Lord. With remarkable humility and an act of generous love, she hastened to perform the work of a servant for Elizabeth. We know how this act of humility affected the infant that was yet to be born: He leaped for joy in the womb of his mother. He is the first human being to acknowledge the coming of Christ. As a result, the Mother of the Lord intoned the beautiful Magnificat with joy, thanksgiving and praise. . . . Mary is an example of how we ought to live, because first and foremost she had welcomed Jesus into her life; then she eagerly hastened to tell the news to her cousin Elizabeth. What she had received, she had to give in turn. (Mother Teresa)

We understand from this that our every action can and ought to be both mission and giving witness, because the world and our neighbors are so much in need of this, but above all they are in need of God who is love.

The beautiful thing about Mary is that when Jesus came into her life, she immediately went in haste to the home of Elizabeth to give Jesus to her and her unborn infant. . . . She did the same thing for the entire world when the Savior was born. (Mother Teresa)

If you want your life to be a true gift, for yourself, for others and for God, then live your life with faith, with love, with understanding and responsibility. Then through you God can be present and operative in the world. What a beautiful mission! What a marvelous thing! What a great responsibility! Such is God's love: He wants to use us in order to be present to others, to save the world by his immense love and pardon!

The world is aware that there was something different—and this was Jesus—in the life of Mother Teresa. The former Secretary-General of the United Nations, Xavier Peres de Cuellar, introduced her to the General Assembly by saying: "I present to you the most powerful woman in the world."

Rajiv Ghandi, the Prime Minister of India, said: "We are proud that Mother Teresa has adopted India as her country. She belongs not only to India, but to the whole world."

Mother Teresa tells us:

The love of God should burst forth as total service.

Jesus Leaves Home

No prophet is without honor except in his native place, indeed, in his own house. And he did not work many miracles there because of their lack of faith.
Matthew 13:57-58

Today, when everything is questioned and everything is changing, let us go back to Nazareth. Jesus came to redeem the world, to teach us about the Father's love.
Mother Teresa

We all prepare ourselves as well as possible for our life and work by means of education and study, so that we can achieve the best within our capability. To leave home and take on responsibility for their lives is a great enterprise for young people. Their new situation requires adjustments and carries with it some risks. They compare themselves to others, become more aware of reality, and are prompted to make choices. That is the beauty of growing up, of maturing within one's environment. Today, however, due to our pluralistic society, culture and religious experience, the passage from one stage of life to another is much more difficult for most people today.

Jesus also passed through the various stages that lead to maturity. Mother Teresa comments on this as follows:

How strange it is that Jesus spent thirty years without doing anything, apparently just wasting time! He had no opportunity to show his personality or his gifts and talents, although we know that at the age of twelve he silenced the learned priests, since he knew so many things and knew them so well. And yet when his parents found him, he returned to Nazareth with them and remained obedient to them. For thirty years we know nothing fur-

ther about him. When he started to publicly teach the people, they were astonished that he, the son of a carpenter, who had worked as a carpenter for thirty years, should do so. (Mother Teresa)

Before beginning his public life, Jesus spent forty days in the desert. While there, he was tempted by the devil, but he firmly rejected the temptations. In so doing, he conquered the devil, and later on he predicted his definitive victory over the devil by his death and resurrection (cf. Lk 4:1-13).

Jesus began his public life very simply in a village of fishermen, as Mark tells us: "Shortly afterward they came to Capernaum, and on the Sabbath he entered the synagogue and began to teach. The people were spellbound by his teaching, because he taught with authority and not like the scribes" (Mk 1:21-22).

The words of Jesus were different from those of other teachers, because Jesus is himself the Word of God. It is God who speaks to us as a man and as a brother. His preaching caused astonishment in the minds of his listeners; they hungered and thirsted for the new doctrine, because he spoke as one who had authority.

Jesus manifested the power of God not only by his words, but also by his deeds, and especially by his miracles. "There appeared in their synagogue a man with an unclean spirit that shrieked: 'What do you want of us, Jesus of Nazareth? Have you come to destroy us? I know who you are—the holy One of God!' Jesus rebuked him sharply: 'Be quiet! Come out of the man!' At that the unclean spirit convulsed the man violently and with a loud shriek came out of him. All who looked on were amazed. They began to ask one another: 'What

does this mean? A completely new teaching in a spirit of authority! He gives orders to unclean spirits and they obey!' From that point on his reputation spread throughout the surrounding region of Galilee" (Mk 1:23-28).

Jesus' first meeting with the people, with the sick and possessed, was full of surprises and novelty, both because of his words and his actions. The enthusiasm, attraction and love for Jesus increased more and more in Capernaum and its surroundings. People were saying: "At last the right man has come to the right place." But instead of responding to their warm reception, openness and friendship, Jesus reacts in a surprising manner that astonishes the crowd.

"Those whom he cured, who were variously afflicted, were many, and so were the demons he expelled. But he would not permit the demons to speak, because they knew him. Rising early the next morning, he went off to a lonely place in the desert; there he was absorbed in prayer. Simon and his companions managed to track him down, and when they found him, they told him: 'Everybody is looking for you!' He said to them: 'Let us move on to the neighboring villages so that I may proclaim the good news there also. That is what I have come to do.' So he went into their synagogues preaching the good news and expelling demons throughout the whole of Galilee" (Mk 1:34-39).

In this way Jesus proclaimed the universality of his mission, the mandate he had received from his Father, and the fundamental importance of the practice of prayer, silence and solitude for the mission of salvation.

Mother Teresa also left her home town of Skopje. Having struggled with her vocation for six years, in the end she submitted.

My family was a happy family, but at the age of eighteen I decided to leave home. Since that time I have never thought to have made a mistake. It was God's will; it was a command more powerful than me. He had chosen me for himself, and I entered the Sisters of Loreto. (Mother Teresa)

Her future mission was one of love in action.

It was a mission of love, of goodness, especially today, when there is such a hunger for God. (Mother Teresa)

Mother Teresa prepared herself for this mission with meticulous care, as Jesus had done, spending years in silence, meditation, prayer and work. This is her testimony:

The years of preparation—the novitiate, followed by the work of teaching as a Sister of Loreto—gave me the opportunity to know and love Jesus more and more.

Each one of us is called to life at birth, to faith at baptism, to goodness, love and happiness by our human nature. What will our life be? What impact will we have on the world? What is the future that awaits us? Surely, it depends on God, on ourselves and on others. Usually, when things go well, we want to take the credit ourselves. But when things go badly, we blame it on God and on others. When we exclude God and others from our life, we remain alone, closed within the circle of our egoism. We no longer live our life; rather, we accept it or submit to it with passive expectation until our ship has run its course.

Silence, prayer and a family that lives in harmony and love are the best preparation for life, as long as the triangle of love—self, God and others—is ever present as we look to the future.

The striving for immediate success, the desire to have everything at once, is a diabolical temptation for many people today, and especially for young people. Jesus' silence for thirty years teaches us instead that we should prepare ourselves seriously and serenely for life, work and family.

Mother Teresa labored in silence in Calcutta for some twenty years. From that hidden life was born the Mother Teresa we all knew: a symbol of faith and love. Every great work is born from silence, prayer, love, suffering and sacrifice. The same is true of an infant, a flower or the fruits of the earth.

The silence that Jesus observed for the thirty years of his life at Nazareth, he continues to observe in the tabernacle, interceding for us. (Mother Teresa)

Jesus Calls

Many people accompanied Jesus in his travels, his activities and encounters, following in his footsteps. Some of them were so committed to Jesus that they had left everyone and everything to follow him, to listen to him, to love him and to assist him. Jesus became for them a new, great and indispensable reality; he was everything to them. These were the disciples of Jesus.

Their community started to form gradually. At first through their listening and reflecting; then they prayed together, and finally the Master openly invited them. They responded with an affirmative decision, accepting him with their hearts and with their lives, collaborating with him as friends. They abandoned themselves to him completely, with a love that ultimately pushed them on to martyrdom.

From the group of his disciples Jesus selected the apostles as his close collaborators in the work of salvation.

One morning he was walking along the shore and a crowd of people was following him. There were numerous fishermen in the crowd and, like the rest of the people, they were hoping for a good day. What would it bring? For some, nothing. It would be a day like so many others: dull, wearisome and fruitless. For others, however, it would be the day of their lives, a day of invitation and mission. This is the way Mark describes it:

"As he made his way along the Sea of Galilee, he observed Simon and his brother Andrew casting their nets into the sea; they were fishermen. Jesus said to them: 'Come after me; I will make you fishers of men.' They immediately abandoned their nets and became his followers. Proceeding a little farther along, he caught sight of James, Zebedee's son, and his brother John. They too were in their boat putting their nets in order. He summoned them on the spot. They abandoned their father Zebedee, who was in the boat with the hired men, and went off in his company" (Mk 1:16-29).

The family of Jesus is a new family, and it has only one purpose: to bear witness to the love of the Father, to call people to conversion and change of life, to a better life of love and pardon.

From among his disciples Jesus tightens the circle even more and selects the apostles who are to represent the twelve tribes of Israel (cf. Lk 6:12-16). Call, choice and vocation spring from our friendship with Jesus, his love for us, and our fascination with his life and new teaching.

No one can be a better friend than Jesus, because his love is so humble, so tender. He is always faithful, even to the point of giving his life for us. (Mother Teresa)

If we read the gospel attentively, we will notice some specific traits in Jesus' selection of his collaborators. After getting to know him closely and receiving a special gift or grace, some of his disciples want to follow Jesus and be with him always, but Jesus does not accept their offer. A typical case is that of the Gerasene demoniac: "The man from whom the devils had departed asked to come with him, but he sent him away with the words: 'Go back home and recount all that God has done for you.' The man went all through the town making public what Jesus had done for him" (Lk 8:38-39).

The mission of the man who was cured is clear and distinct: He is to bear witness to the works of God.

Some disciples, on the other hand, were called by Jesus himself, but they were not ready to abandon everything and everyone in order to follow Jesus and live for him alone. Such was the case of the rich young man, who was already living an exemplary life. For this reason, Jesus loved him and invited him to strive for perfection by offering him a test, a choice between wealth and Jesus: "If you seek perfection, go, sell your possessions, and give them to the poor. You will then have treasure in heaven. Afterward, come back and follow me" (Mt 19:21).

A clean cut, a radical and difficult choice. Unfortunately, it was the wealth that prevailed: "Hearing these words, the young man went away sad, for his possessions were many" (Mt 19:22). He was unable to understand and to choose Jesus as his greatest treasure in life. Consequently, he could not give up everything in order to assist the poor; he could not willingly accept and live discipleship for Jesus. "Jesus said to his disciples: 'I assure you, only with difficulty will a rich man enter into the kingdom of God'" (Mt 19:23).

Commenting on the scarcity of religious vocations, Mother Teresa said:

I think that the reason why there are no vocations in the Church today, or they are few in number, is due in part to the fact that there is too much wealth, too much comfortable living, a standard of living that is too high, not only in families but also in religious life itself. . . . We are only little pencils in the hand of God. He writes what he wants.

On one occasion Mother Teresa told me:

In our Congregation we have Sisters from every part of the world. Some of them come from families that are wealthy and very well off. When they come to us, they persevere and are content with our life. I myself ask them: "Why do you want to remain with us?" And for sure the immediate reply is: "Because of Jesus, and because of our poverty." They tell me: "Mother, we want only one wealth—Jesus— and we are happy to have found a Congregation that is poor and depends entirely on divine providence."

Wealth in itself is good, if it is used well. The rich young man in the gospel had the opportunity to assist the poor, and then he could have taken the next step: to follow Jesus. But he did not do so. When wealth becomes our goal in life, instead of being only a means, we lose our freedom and are in danger of losing our soul as well.

An Albanian proverb carries the voice of experience: "Wealth is a good servant but a bad master."

Mother Teresa had a vocation within a vocation or, as they say, "a second calling." She said:

My specific vocation is for the poor among the poorest of the poor. And it was not easy. . . . A house was needed in which to

gather the abandoned. I started to look for one. . . . I walked and walked until I could go no farther. I then understood better how much the poor suffer; always in search of food, medicine, everything. The memory of the material comfort I enjoyed in the convent of Loreto was like a temptation for me. I prayed: "My God, by my free choice and for love of you I want to remain here and do whatever your divine will asks of me. The poor are my community. Their security is mine. Their health is mine. The new house will be the house of the poor."

Then, speaking of her vocation, she said:

We live and work for God through our consecration, striving to witness God's love to the poor, and especially to those who are suffering. . . . Our vocation is holiness. . . . We all have the duty of serving God wherever we are: in our family, at work, in school, in the hospital, wherever.

She is not speaking here specifically of a religious vocation, but of the human and Christian vocation that applies to all. For we are all called to life, to faith, and to the love that places us at the service of others. As he did in the gospel, so also today, Jesus calls us to life, to life with others and for others, to life with God in faith and love. Some do not experience it because they do not know of it. Others do experience it and understand it partially, but they do not commit themselves to it. Unfortunately, only a few, today as then, accept the invitation of Jesus to live, to love, to give witness to life and to God's love for us.

You, too, should think of this. You are alive;

therefore you are called to life. You are baptized; therefore you are called to the new life of faith, to live in communion with God and neighbor. You are also called to a step further, to perfection, to the total giving of self to Christ, neighbor, and Church.

By reason of a vocation fully accepted and lived, Mother Teresa has brought very much good to the world! But we too should be able to say with conviction and with Christian joy: God is present in our world! He loves us and he calls us!

Mother Teresa as a young girl

Jesus and Children

Let the children come to me
and do not hinder them. . . .
I assure you that whoever does not accept
the reign of God like a little child
shall not take part in it.
Mark 10:14-15

If there is so much suffering and sadness
in the world today, it is because the child,
the unborn child, the innocent child
is unwanted, rejected, neglected. . . .
A child is God's greatest gift to the family,
to the nation, to the world.
The child is a life from God,
created in the image of God,
created for great things:
to love and be loved.
Mother Teresa

Very quickly Jesus was highly esteemed and loved by the people. He was constantly surrounded by the sick and the possessed, by friends including women, and very often also by children. He was friendly to everyone, but especially to children. He approached them, embraced them, loved them and spoke with them.

This behavior seemed out of place to the apostles, as if it were not serious enough or not worthy of him. They considered it to be a waste of time or even as something that could compromise the Master, the apostles, and his entire mission.

"People were bringing their little children to him to have him touch them, but the disciples were scolding them for this. Jesus became indignant when he noticed it and said to them: 'Let the children come to me and do not hinder them. It is to just such as these that the kingdom of God belongs. I assure you that whoever does not accept the reign of God like a little child shall not take part in it.' Then he embraced them and blessed them, placing his hands on them" (Mk 10:13-16).

Jesus not only loved the children but went further, stipulating a condition that applied to everybody: It is necessary to become like a child to enter the kingdom of heaven. The phrase "like a child" means here to be innocent, simple, open, genuine and good.

On another occasion Jesus caused even greater astonishment to his disciples, the people around him, and also to his enemies by a statement that was much more startling. This is how he answered the question presented by his disciples as to who was the greatest in the kingdom of God: "He called a little child over and stood him in their midst and said: 'I assure you, unless you change and become like little children, you will not enter the kingdom of God'" (Mt 18:2-3).

Then he immediately explained why he had stipulated this condition: "Whoever makes himself lowly, becoming like this child, is of greatest importance in that heavenly reign. Whoever welcomes one such child for my sake welcomes me" (Mt 18:4-5).

By this kindly and surprising gesture, Jesus gives value to that which is disdained, namely, the child. He praises that which has little value in the eyes of many: the lowliness of children. He identifies with them, thus opening a completely new horizon for life and for the kingdom of heaven.

Unfortunately, in many societies today children are again considered superfluous, a burden. They are an obstacle to the enjoyment of life, to one's career or financial gain, to one's freedom and autonomy. They are a source of worry and preoccupation! The industrial and post-industrial society has embraced certain values that are opposed to life. They destroy the new life of the infant by abortion; they marginalize the elderly out of the family and out of society by putting them in nursing homes. They want only the best years of life—youth and maturity—and they want to eliminate the life of the unborn, of infants and the elderly.

We have reached the ultimate absurdity of egoism, which kills and destroys everything that is not a source of pleasure, wealth or comfort. As a result, life is shattered, disdained and, in many instances, destroyed. This is a manifestation of a fear of life and a fear of death!

When Mother Teresa received the Nobel Peace Prize in Oslo in 1979, she said:

Abortion is the greatest danger to peace. I believe that no human hand should ever be raised to kill life. Every life is God's life within us. Even the unborn child has God's life within itself. We have no right to destroy this life, whatever the means we use to do so. . . . An infant is always a gift from God.

The absurdity is even more serious when we consider that it is in the wealthy countries that abortion is practiced the most.

In my opinion, if abortion is permitted in wealthy countries that have all the means that money can buy, those countries are the poorest among the poor. . . . So many infants today are in the category of the unwanted, the unloved. . . . It is a wonderful thing when an infant has been able to escape death at the hands of parents who have welcomed it. . . . This is one of the most admirable characteristics of our people, namely, their willingness to adopt and to offer a home and love to these unwanted babies; to Christ in the likeness of the infants. (Mother Teresa)

Some people think they have done their human and Christian duty if they have chosen life, a baby, without doing much more, that is, without giving them love and a good education, without giving of themselves.

Today the world of the wealthy is risking self-destruction because of abortion, low birth rates, the war against life and love, and immorality.

To babies and to the poor, to all who are suffering and alone, give the gift of a smile; give them not only your care but your heart as well.

It is a noteworthy thing that God should have chosen an unborn baby to give witness to him before the birth of Jesus, but it is sad to think of all the infants that are unborn today through the choice of their parents. . . . Abortion is the greatest danger to peace, because we are able to destroy the life that is given by God. If a mother can become the murderer of her children, what can we say about other kinds of murders and wars in the world? People today no longer love one another, and it is precisely here that the danger to peace lies. Abortion is the source of the evils in the world. (Mother Teresa)

Let us return to the beginning. Jesus asks us to become like little children and to welcome every child as if it were Jesus himself. This is the condition for entering the kingdom of heaven, that is, for our salvation.

How can one welcome the infant Jesus if one does not even accept the fruit of love, the new life of unborn infants? The destruction of life that is abortion leads to the destruction of faith and of love. At the same time it is also proof of an already existing lack of faith and love. God has created us to be bearers of life, of love, and of joy; to be signs of his presence in the world. Whoever is an instrument of death through abortion or through the marginalization and abandonment of the elderly, cannot be a witness to Jesus, who is life. He is doing the work of Herod, of the devil, and not of God.

Therefore, by our attitude toward life we reveal our attitude toward faith, our relationship to God and to neighbor.

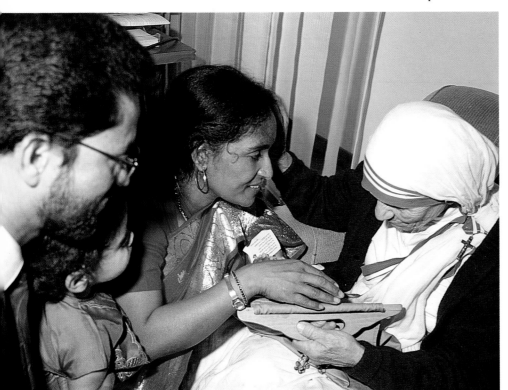

There is a hunger for ordinary bread. But there is also a hunger for love, for goodness, for friendship, life and caring. This is the great poverty that causes so much suffering for so many people.

O God, give us the grace to stop the killing of babies in their mother's womb all over the world. Most holy Mother Mary, you who welcomed Jesus with such great love, aid and protect all mothers throughout the world against the sin of abortion! (Mother Teresa)

Jesus and the Sick

The spirit of the Lord is upon me;
therefore he has anointed me.
He has sent me
to bring glad tidings to the poor,
to proclaim liberty to captives,
recovery of sight to the blind
and release to prisoners,
to announce a year of favor from the Lord.
Luke 4:18-19

My community is the poor;
their security is mine, their health is mine.
My house is the house of the poor;
not only of the poor,
but of the poorest of the poor;
those whom no one will approach
because they are contagious,
full of germs and filth;
those who do not go to pray because
they cannot go out of their homes naked;
those who do not eat because
they no longer have the strength to eat;
those who collapse on the sidewalk,
knowing that they are about to die,
while the pedestrians pass them by
without looking back;
those who do not weep
because they have no more tears.
Mother Teresa

Sickness is a part of life, and it can be present at any phase or age—in infancy, adolescence, maturity or old age. Besides the pain, a sick person suffers also from loneliness, from the feeling of being useless to family and society, of being a burden. To be sick today means to be isolated and in many cases abandoned. This augments the suffering and causes unnecessary pain.

Mother Teresa once confided to me:

There are so many hospitals and so many kinds of medicine in the world today, but there is very little loving care for the sick. The sick are in need of everything but especially of attention and love. We give ourselves to them through our care, but we would also like to help them recognize and love in us the source of love who is God.

Although there has been a great deal of progress in medicine in our days, the hospitals are still crowded. Many stay there only for a while and then return home cured. Others remain in hospitals or nursing homes for many years without knowing what the future will bring; and some die there.

Even people in good health live with the constant prospect of ending up in the hospital one day. Since sickness is considered an inevitable evil, people will do anything to take care of their health.

In Jesus' time sickness was seen as a punishment from God for a person's sins or those of his or her ancestors. This mentality made sickness more difficult, and even traumatic.

But Jesus had a very different attitude. He extended special care to the marginalized and underprivileged: the sick, the poor, sinners, and children. Here is a typical example:

"He then left Tyrian territory and returned by way of Sidon to the Sea of Galilee, into the district of the Ten Cities. Some people brought him a deaf man who had a speech impediment and begged him to lay his hand on him. Jesus took him off by himself away from the crowd. He put his fingers into the man's ears and, spitting, touched his tongue; then he looked up to heaven and emitted a groan. He said to him: 'Ephphatha!' (that is, 'Be opened!'). At once the man's ears were opened; he was freed from the impediment and began to speak plainly" (Mk 7:31-35).

The cure caused great astonishment in the people and they testified: "He has done everything well! He makes the deaf hear and the mute speak!" (Mk 7:37). What a marvelous testimony: to say that he has done all things well! After observing our life and actions, could people say the same?

The gospel records many other incidents in which Jesus shows empathy for the suffering of the sick, takes care of them and treats them lovingly. In some cases he intervenes miraculously and thereby helps people believe. Cures and healing are a sign of the presence and power of God, of the salvation and freedom that Jesus brings.

"Jesus continued his tour of all the towns and villages. He taught in their synagogues, he proclaimed the good news of God's reign, and he cured every sickness and disease" (Mt 9:35; cf. Acts 10:38).

The Church, all of us, should have the same attitude toward the sick. We should strive to be close to those who suffer, so that we can assist them by our solidarity and our love.

Jesus also said this: "Come! You have my Father's blessing! Inherit the kingdom prepared for you from the creation of the world. For I was hungry and you gave me food, I was thirsty and you gave me drink. I was a stranger and you welcomed me, naked and you clothed me. I was ill and you comforted me, in prison and you came to visit me. . . . I assure you, as often as you did it for one of my least brothers, you did it for me" (Mt 25:34-40).

Thus, Jesus identifies with everyone who suffers. To enter into the kingdom of heaven and attain salvation, he asks us to love and serve him in the person of our neighbor in need. At the last judgment, our salvation or eternal condemnation will depend on this: Whether we have or have not recognized, loved and served Jesus in our neighbor who is suffering!

It is this statement of Jesus that has inspired the entire life and work of Mother Teresa. Referring to their work with the dying and especially with lepers, she said:

If our Sisters did not see the face of Jesus in these unfortunate persons, this kind of work would be impossible. . . . We want them to know that there are persons who truly love them, and even more, that God loves them very much. (Mother Teresa)

Speaking later about the time spent caring for the needy, Mother Teresa said:

All my time belongs to others, because in dedicating myself with all my heart to the suffering, it is Jesus whom we serve in his disfigured face, for he himself has said: "You have done it for me."

We Christians are called to look at life not superficially but to profoundly evaluate through our God-given faith the meaning of life and of everything that surrounds us. Faith opens not only our eyes but also our hearts to love and service, thus making our life a gift for others.

Our criterion for assistance is not one's belief, but one's need. All are the body of Christ; all are Christ under the appearance of those in need of assistance and love, and they have a right to receive it. (Mother Teresa)

Hence, sickness gives us a chance not only to do good to the sick by visiting them and caring for them, but to give witness to our love for Jesus himself. It is an occasion to verify whether or not we truly believe in, live and love God.

"The Church encompasses with her love all those who are afflicted by human misery, and she recognizes in those who are poor and who suffer the image of her poor and suffering founder. She does all in her power to relieve their need, and in them she strives to serve Christ" (LG 8).

This great opportunity and mission must never be wasted or underestimated. Rather, it should be carried out with meticulous care, with an appreciation for the value of suffering and love.

There are medicines and cures for almost every kind of sickness. But there are not willing hands to serve and generous hearts to love. I think that it is impossible to cure the terrible sickness of not feeling loved. . . . No sickness, not even leprosy, can so disfigure the human face that one cannot see in it a neighbor, and even more, the face of the suffering Jesus. (Mother Teresa)

Jesus and Sinners

*God did not send the Son into the world
to condemn the world, but that the world
might be saved through him.*

John 3:17

*Jesus can pardon much
because he loves much.
Great love can pardon a great sin.
As it is with Jesus,
it should also be with us:
If we truly want to pardon,
we must love truly.*

Mother Teresa

We are both strong and weak, mortal and immortal, spiritual and carnal, inclined to good and also to evil. These tendencies create an internal conflict in us: Can I or can't I, should I or shouldn't I, do I want to or not want to, does it serve my purpose or not?

We experience within ourselves many aspirations, desires and intentions. Some of them are those of everyday life; others are greater in scope; still others are beyond our possibility or capability and hence cannot be realized.

But our pride does not permit us to admit our limitations, and much less to admit that we need others to realize our capabilities. Still less do we want to admit that without God we are lost, discontent, and deluded. Something similar results from the experience of sin, wherein we manifest our human weakness, our limitations, our inability to choose and do good and to avoid evil.

"For when man looks into his own heart he finds that he is drawn toward what is wrong and sunk in many evils which cannot come from his good Creator. . . . Man therefore is divided in himself. As a result, the whole life of men, both individual and social, shows itself to be a struggle, and a dramatic one, between good and evil, between light and darkness" (GS 13).

This experience caused Paul to write as follows: "I know that no good dwells in me, that is, in my flesh; the desire to do right is there but not the power. What happens is that I do, not the good I will to do, but the evil I do not intend" (Rm 7:18-19). In this interior warfare, everyone needs to be helped and supported with love in order to increase the good and lessen the evil.

The greatest sin is the lack of love or charity, the terrible indifference toward one's neighbor who, on the curb of the street, falls victim to exploitation, corruption, indigence and sickness. (Mother Teresa)

Jesus became man to help us in this interior struggle. What is more, by his love, his forgiveness, his death and resurrection, he has freed us from the slavery of sin and death. In his life and works Jesus had a particular predilection for sinners, trying in this way to sustain the good in every person and cast out the evil. He said publicly: "The Son of Man has come to search out and save what was lost" (Lk 19:10).

The choice of good or evil in a human being depends on many internal and external factors, but especially on how we use our freedom. "It is, however, only in freedom that man can turn himself toward what is good. The people of our time prize freedom very highly and strive eagerly for it. In this they are right. Yet, they often cherish it improperly, as if it gave them leave to do anything they like, even when it is evil. But that which is truly freedom is an exceptional sign of the image of God in man. . . . Man's dignity therefore requires him to act out of conscious and free choice, as moved and drawn in a personal way from within, and not by blind impulses in himself or by mere external constraint. . . . Since human freedom has been weakened by sin, it is only by the help of God's grace that man can give his actions their full and proper relationship to God" (GS 17).

The key to this change and improvement is Jesus. We need to open ourselves to him and collaborate with him, and not give in to evil. We need to believe in Jesus and his victory, which becomes our true freedom, our true happiness, our true life and assurance. Only Jesus can guarantee complete freedom that sustains the good in us, makes it increase, mature, and thus renders us capable of collaborating with others.

It is wonderful to realize that in spite of our sins God does not despair of us. Rather, the weaker we are, the more he loves us. Because he knows very well that his grace arouses in us "any measure of desire or achievement" (Phil 2:13).

Unfortunately today, after two thousand years, many either do not know or do not want to know that in Jesus lies our only real chance to become new. In him we become free and capable of loving and pardoning, suffering and rejoicing, believing in and giving witness to a new humanity, a new family and a new society (cf. GS 22).

Sad to say, some people see Jesus as a restriction, an obstacle to their freedom and their achievements. He is seen as a rival, or worse, as someone who wants to condemn us to slavery. Those who think this way, believe to find freedom in evil, in sin, in the opportunity to do whatever pleases them and makes them comfortable.

And yet, the experience of sin and of pardon is part of our life of faith. Mother Teresa said:

Sin pursues us and is present within us, but we should never despair. We should never become discouraged. . . . None of this is necessary if we have understood the tenderness of God's love. We are precious to him because he loves us; he loves us so tenderly that he has cupped us in the palms of his hands. When your heart is restless, when your heart is in pain, when your heart feels as if it is breaking . . . then remember this: "I am precious in his sight; he loves me. He has called me by name. I am his. God loves me. To show his love, Jesus died on the cross."

In the struggle against sin we are never alone.

Jesus is always with us, as is the Christian community and God's grace. With humility and love we can always move forward in our search for good, freedom, and perfection.

The only power that can change us is love, that is, God. If it is true that sin and evil are a reality, even more so is the redemption brought by Christ. So why stop at the first step, that of evil, instead of humbly and lovingly advancing with Jesus to the very end? We are capable of overcoming evil, slavery and sin. If the reality of sin is difficult and depressing, more beautiful and consoling by far is the reality of pardon and love: JESUS!

Jesus and His Friends

I no longer speak of you as slaves,
for a slave does not know
what his master is about.
Instead I call you friends,
since I have made known to you
all that I heard from my Father.
John 15:15

I live with Jesus and for Jesus
for twenty-four hours of the day;
I offer him my life, my heart,
my love, my work, everything.
Mother Teresa

Friendship is a very great good, a gift that we should accept and reciprocate with gratitude. A friend is one who understands and accepts us, wishes us well, remains faithful to us and is always willing to give us a hand. Who has friends is usually more secure, stronger, and more at peace, not relying only on him or herself, but also on others. The invisible but strong network of relationships based on friendship makes our lives happy and more open, more disposed for good, more generous.

Of all the persons that we have met, some have made only a slight impression on us and perhaps are now forgotten. They may have left a pleasant memory but nothing more. But there are others who remain with us. To some extent they become part of our thoughts, our plans, our commitments and the things we hold dear. They have penetrated to the depths of our being, and if for the moment they are far away, even if we do not expect to meet them again, they mean a great deal to us.

Such persons are friends. They have shared something of themselves with us, and perhaps we too have given them something lasting. As a result, a union has been established that transcends time.

In our world deep friendships are usually rare. Our relationships are often transient and formal, resulting more from our task in society than from personal intimacy. But precisely for this reason we feel a stronger need for friendship and interpersonal relationships. We want to be understood, accepted as we are, and encourage one another as we walk on our common path. Among friends, we can be ourselves, express ourselves without any pretense. At the same time we can develop freely, even revealing the limitations and defects that we normally conceal.

Jesus also had friends. He conversed with them; he spent more time with them than with others; he explained his plans to them; they traveled and lived together. He made them understand in numerous ways that he truly accepted them, held them in high regard, loved and trusted them. He did not choose them because they belonged to any specific social class or because they had any particular gift or merit. He chose them because they were who they were. So in turn they loved him and followed him for who he was.

In addition to Jesus' friendship with the twelve apostles, the gospels speak in particular about his friendship with Lazarus and Lazarus' sisters, Martha and Mary. He often spent time in their home for moments of relaxation and joy.

The relationship between Jesus and Martha and Mary is especially interesting. Mary did not know at what hour Jesus would arrive, but while he was there she would stay close to him, listening to him and enjoying his presence. Martha, on the other hand, would busy herself with welcoming him and preparing lunch or supper as soon as he arrived. This was her way of showing how happy she was and how much she loved the Master.

But when Martha asks Jesus to scold her sister for leaving her alone to do the serving, she is the one who receives a scolding: "Martha, Martha, you are anxious and upset about many things; one thing only is required. Mary has chosen the better portion and she shall not be deprived of it" (Lk 10:41-42).

With this unexpected response Jesus wants to send a message to all of us: The primary and essential characteristic of our friendship with him is the attention we pay to his word and his presence. To be with him, to listen to him, to speak to him: These are the things that we should value the most; they are "the better portion." Works are also important and necessary, but they come later. The person in the Church who has the gift of contemplation should not be considered useless or lazy; in fact, it is the contemplatives who remind us of what is essential in our relationship with God. Martha does well to serve Jesus, to prepare food for him and his disciples, but Mary does better by remaining in his presence and giving him her complete attention.

Mother Teresa said:

We are active contemplatives in the world; we live entirely for Jesus. We find him and love and serve him first of all in the eucharist, in prayer, in meditation, and then in persons who are suffering. If it were not for our faith, our love and service for our neighbor would be impossible.

I once asked her: "How is it possible to correlate action and contemplation, the spiritual life and the various pastoral ministries today?" Mother Teresa answered:

We do everything for Jesus. You are a priest of Christ. . . . Let Jesus grow in you with his love. Then everything will be easier for you, because you will live for Jesus and also work for Jesus. Action without meditation, without prayer and a spiritual life, is suicide for our faith and love. If you are supposed to bring Jesus to others, how much you must live in him, love him and be close to him. . . . Today Jesus continues to suffer in you, in me, in the youth of the world. He is re-living his passion. To recognize this means to have faith, to love, to bear witness of Jesus to others.

Another page of the gospel surprises us and leaves us puzzled: Jesus is speaking to the people when someone comes forward to tell him that his mother and brothers are outside waiting to speak to him.

"He said to the one who had told him: 'Who is my mother? Who are my brothers?' Then extending his hand toward his disciples, he said: 'These are my mother and my brothers. Whoever does the will of my heavenly Father is brother and sister and mother to me'" (Mt 12:48-50).

It would seem that Jesus had little regard for his mother and his relatives, but such was not the case. He was simply taking the occasion to give us a strong and clear message: Who wants to be my friend, my brother, sister or mother, must do the will of my Father. That is the essential condition for being a friend of Jesus.

At the Last Supper Jesus said: "If you love me and obey the commands I give you, I will ask the Father and he will give you another Paraclete" (Jn 14:15-16). To speak today of "doing God's will" and "obeying the commandments" may seem irrelevant and far re-

moved from the notion of friendship. But Jesus did say: "As the Father has loved me, so I have loved you. Live on in my love. You will live in my love if you keep my commandments, even as I have kept my Father's commandments, and live in his love " (Jn 15:9-10).

It is friendship, therefore, and love that enables us to know and observe the commandments, to live according to the faith, and to love the Father whom Jesus has revealed to us. The greatest proof of Jesus' love for his disciples is revelation. He opened his heart to them and disclosed the mystery of God. "There is no greater love than this: to lay down one's life for one's friends."

Jesus gave his life for us; and we should give our lives for him, in accordance with his command: "Love one another as I have loved you" (Jn 15:12).

All those who have believed in Jesus have accepted him as Lord, master, redeemer, friend and brother. Our life of union with Jesus began at baptism, was nourished through the sacraments of penance and the eucharist, and ought always to grow and reach maturity.

These are the pillars of friendship with Jesus:

— to remain with him, as Mary did, which we do by praying, meditating and receiving the sacraments;

— to do his Father's will, which we do through the obedience of faith, by our constant search for God's will, avoiding sin, and cultivating the interior life in the Holy Spirit;

— to love one another as he loved us, which requires fraternal union and sharing, mutual pardon, fidelity to the Church, dialogue, works of charity and service to one another.

On these pillars our friendship with Jesus will be firm and secure; and even if one or all of them should collapse because of our weakness, we can be certain that his friendship for us remains unchanged. He has said "You are my friends," and he will never go back on his word.

In the light of charity . . . we should help Jesus to bring a multitude of the poor to union with the Church and with God, for their own salvation and for the greater glory of God. (Mother Teresa)

"There is no greater love than this: to lay down one's life for one's friends."

Jesus and the People

People always seem to need a sure guide to a better future. Among the people of Israel this task was first entrusted to the judges, then to the king, and finally to the prophets, who spoke and taught the people in the name of God.

Jesus is the greatest of all the prophets. He is also God who became man in order to dwell among us. His manner of speaking of the Father, his works, and especially his miracles, aroused in the people great enthusiasm, confidence, and love. They could confess with conviction and joy: "He is the Messiah, the Promised One!"

People followed him faithfully and everywhere, and sometimes it reached a point when they forgot everything else—time and place and even to eat and drink. They wanted only to be close to him, to listen to him, to touch him, to have him in their midst (cf. Lk 9:12-17).

The difference between Jesus and the other prophets was evident to all. Jesus spoke in the name of the heavenly Father and not only in the name of the Mosaic Law, as the scribes did. He spoke with authority, and he worked effectively for their salvation and liberation. The first proof of the change, of the freedom that he brought them, were his miracles. Freeing people of their illnesses was already an indication of freedom from evil and slavery, a sign of salvation.

"He was teaching in their synagogues, and all were loud in his praise. He came to Nazareth where he had been reared and, entering the synagogue on the Sabbath, as he was in the habit of doing, he stood up to do the reading. When the book of the prophet Isaiah was handed him, he unrolled the scroll and found the passage where it was written: 'The spirit of the Lord is upon me; therefore he has anointed me. He has sent me to bring glad tidings to the poor, to proclaim liberty to captives, recovery of sight to the blind, and release to prisoners, to announce a year of favor from the Lord'" (Lk 4:15-19).

People were happy with the novelty of Jesus' presence among them. This was perhaps best expressed by the woman who cried out in the name of the people: "Blest is the womb that bore you and the breasts that nursed you" (Lk 11:27).

People were enthusiastic and ran after him, because they felt that here at last was a new teaching. "People were coming and going in great numbers, making it impossible for them to so much as eat. So Jesus and the apostles went off in a boat by themselves to a deserted place. People saw them leaving, and many got to know about it. People from all the towns hastened on foot to the place, arriving ahead of them" (Mk 6:21-33).

Starting with the people of Israel, through his teaching Jesus created a new people of God, made up of believers and the redeemed, people from every tongue, nation, culture and time. "If they are consecrated a kingly priesthood and a holy nation (cf. 1 Pt 2:4-10), it is in order that they may in all their actions offer spiritual sacrifices and bear witness to Christ all the world over" (AA 3). "But all the members, many though they are, are one body" (1 Cor 12:12).

Today this new people of God is the Church. She gathers all members together, gives them life and nourishes them through the presence of Christ in our midst, especially in the eucharist. Today as then Christ teaches and nourishes us through his Church to lead us to salvation.

In carrying on the work of Christ, the Church teaches his doctrine with authority. And then, with patience and love, she leads us to the Promised Land of salvation, guiding us step by step throughout our lives.

I once asked Mother Teresa: "What is your method of working with the poor?" She answered:

We search for them everywhere. In some cases the people in the vicinity bring them to us; sometimes the police do, because everybody knows us, and they know that we work for these people and welcome them wholeheartedly. Out of love we call them "our people," and other persons will speak of them as "Mother Teresa's people." We should all learn how to love without discrimination.

To Pray with Jesus

When he had sent them away,
he went up on the mountain to pray,
remaining there alone as evening drew on.
Matthew 14:23-24

There is only one powerful prayer;
there is only one voice that rises up
from the face of the earth;
it is the voice of Christ.
The more we receive in our silent prayer,
the more we can give in our active life.
Mother Teresa

ll four evangelists speak of Jesus praying in various circumstances of his life on earth. For example, "Rising early the next morning, he went off to a lonely place in the desert; there he was absorbed in prayer" (Mk 1:35). "He often retired to deserted places and prayed" (Lk 5:16). "Then he went out to the mountain to pray, spending the night in communion with God" (Lk 6:12).

What is the reason for Jesus' "need" to draw apart and pray? It comes from his love for his Father, his desire to be with him. Prayer is an opening up to God, an important moment in our dialogue of love with God, a direct communication between him and ourselves.

Do we know how to put everything aside in order to remain alone with God? Frequently we can find a thousand excuses for not praying: our work, our family or even our works of charity. "I don't have time" is an excuse that we commonly use; it seems to fit every circumstance. But if we look at it more closely, it means "I don't feel the need to pray," or even "It seems to be such a waste of time." There are so many other things that are more important, more interesting, more profitable, more . . .

Jesus had admonished Martha, "Only one thing is necessary," and it is this: our union with

God. From this our life and activities derive direction.

Joy is prayer.
Joy is power.
Joy is love.
Joy is a net of love for winning over souls. . . .
To be joyful in Christ and then to work and live
*   for him means:*
To love as he loved,
To help as he helped,
To give as he gave,
To save as he saved,
To be with him
twenty-four hours a day. . . .
Without prayer there is no faith.
Without faith there is no love.
Without love there is no self-giving.
Without self-giving there is no service
to those who are in need. (Mother Teresa)

Many people today ask: "What can I do? The rhythm of life puts us under great pressure. I do everything in haste and end up even praying in haste."

At first glance this seems to be true. But at close look, the wrong reasoning becomes evident. More importantly, if our life is really like this, it is utterly distorted. If they are not accompanied by prayer, if they are not the *fruit* of our prayer and our love of God and neighbor, our efforts and sacrifices quickly lead to a false life.

Was not Jesus busy from morning until night? Did they not say to him: "Everybody is looking for you" (Mk 1:37)? But he did not lessen his prayer on that account; rather, he increased it. His practice of prayer prompted the apostles to be more reflective. It aroused in them a desire to pray. In fact, they soon asked him: "Lord, teach us to pray" (Lk 11:1).

Jesus willingly responded to the request and started to teach them about prayer. This is necessary for us as well. In the Our Father, Jesus teaches us the fundamental themes of prayer:

— glorification of the name of God;

— the coming of his kingdom and the fulfillment of his will;

— daily bread, both material and spiritual, for all people;

— forgiveness of sin;

— protection against evil.

When the disciples asked Jesus to teach them how to pray, he answered: "When you pray, say: Our Father . . ." He did not teach them any particular method or technique. He simply said that we should pray to God as our Father, as a loving Father. I have said to the bishops that the disciples had seen the Master pray many times, even for entire nights. The people should see you pray and recognize you as men of prayer. Then they will listen to you when you speak to them about prayer. . . . We have such a need of prayer in order to be able to see Christ in the afflicted countenances of the poorest of the poor. . . . Speak to God; let God speak to you; let Jesus pray in you. To pray means to speak with God. He is my Father. Jesus is my all. (Mother Teresa)

In Jesus' teaching the link between prayer and communion is very important. "Again I tell you, if two of you join your voices on earth to pray for anything whatever, it shall be granted you by my Father in heaven. Where two or three are gathered in my name, there am I in their midst" (Mt 18:19-20).

Another important element is forgiveness. "When you stand to pray, forgive anyone against whom you have a grievance, so that your heavenly Father may in turn forgive you your faults" (Mk 11:25).

We now come to the highest point of prayer, that which best qualifies it as Christian prayer, namely, that it must always be made in Jesus' name. "Whatever you ask in my name I will do, so as to glorify the Father in the Son. Anything you ask me in my name I will do" (Jn 14:13-14).

This means to pray "in him," to be one with him. As the liturgy has it, "Through him, with him, in him, in the unity of the Holy Spirit, all glory and honor is yours, almighty Father, for ever and ever." This is the very heart of liturgical prayer.

If you want to pray better, you should pray more. . . . The time that we spend in daily prayer with God is the most precious part of the whole day. . . . Prayer helps us to know and do the will of God. . . . God is a friend of silence. We have to find God, but we cannot find him in the midst of noise and agitation. . . . If we really want to pray, we must above all dispose ourselves to listen, because in the silence of the heart the Lord speaks. (Mother Teresa)

To Love as Jesus Loved

Jesus said to him: "You shall love the Lord your God with your whole heart, with your whole soul, and with all your mind." This is the greatest and first commandment. The second is like it: "You shall love your neighbor as yourself." On these two commandments the whole law is based, and the prophets as well.

Matthew 22:37-40

It is through love of God and of neighbor that one arrives at complete happiness, at total service without limits, thus giving God to others, a God of peace, a living God, a God of love.

Mother Teresa

To love as Jesus loved. But is this possible? The very title arouses in our minds perplexity and doubt, not to mention incredulity. Even worse, it can cause a sense of something impossible, a feeling of hopelessness that leads to indifference.

Hidden within us there are so many questions that can be expressed in this way: Whom did Jesus love? How did Jesus love? Why did Jesus love?

Jesus is love incarnate, God made man, and therefore his first love is for his Father. "The man without love has known nothing of God, for God is love. God's love was revealed in our midst in this way: He sent his only Son to the world that we might have life through him" (1 Jn 4:8-9).

Jesus taught us: "'You shall love the Lord your God with your whole heart, with your whole soul, and with all your mind.' This is the greatest and first commandment" (Mt 22:37-38).

Immediately after love of God comes love of neighbor. "The second is like it: 'You shall love your neighbor as yourself.' On these two commandments the whole law is based, and the prophets as well" (Mt 22:39-40).

"The dignity of man rests above all on the fact that he is called to communion with God. The invitation to converse with God is addressed to man as soon as he comes into being. For if man exists it is because God has created him through love, and through love continues to hold him in existence. He cannot live fully according to the truth unless he freely acknowledges that love and entrusts himself to his Creator" (GS 19).

"Love of God and one's neighbor, then, is the first and greatest commandment. . . . It goes without saying that this is a matter of the utmost importance to men who are coming to rely more and more on each other and to a world which is becoming more unified every day" (GS 24).

If we may put it this way, the "third commandment of love" which Jesus taught us is love for one's enemies. "You have heard the commandment: 'You shall love your countryman but hate your enemy.' My command to you is: love your enemies, pray for your persecutors. This will prove that you are sons of your heavenly Father, for his sun rises on the bad and the good, he rains on the just and the unjust. If you love those who love you, what merit is there in that? Do not tax collectors do as much? And if you greet your brothers only, what is so praiseworthy about that? Do not pagans do as much? In a word, you must be made perfect as your heavenly Father is perfect" (Mt 4:43-48).

There is something new in the second commandment of love for one's neighbor. Jesus expressed it this way: "I give you a new commandment: Love one another. Such as my love has been for you, so must your love be for each other. This is how all will know you for my disciples: your love for one another" (Jn 13:34-35).

It is the "third law of love" that is the most difficult; it goes against our wishes and seems to be beyond human possibility. Nevertheless, it is a law that is truly divine and supernatural.

Jesus not only commanded love of neighbor; he himself practiced it perfectly. In the dramatic moment of his agony on the cross, he did not think of himself; he prayed for his enemies: "Father, forgive them; they do not know what they are doing" (Lk 23:34).

Paul writes: "Bless your persecutors; bless and do not curse them" (Rm 12:14). Then he gives this testimony: "We work hard at manual labor. When we are insulted we respond with a blessing. Persecution comes our way; we bear it patiently. We are slandered, and we try conciliation" (1 Cor 4:12-13).

What is new in all this is not so much the message, the commandment, but the imitation of Jesus: to love as Jesus loves. This is the sign by which we can recognize his disciples throughout the world.

Mother Teresa gave this testimony:

The poor are a gift from God; they are who we love the most. Christ will not ask us how much we have done, but how much love we have put into our actions. Keep the light of Christ burning in your hearts. He alone is the way to follow. He is the truth that we must speak. He is the love that we must love.

Mother Teresa's whole life and work can be summarized in this:

All that we do is for Jesus, with Jesus and offered to Jesus.

For Jesus: Our whole life is directed to him, to his service; we live only for him, to love and serve him, to make him known and loved.

With Jesus: He gives us the strength, the

comfort, the happiness of working for him; he accompanies us on our way; he leads and guides us; we are with Jesus on the road to Emmaus, where we have recognized him.

Offered to Jesus: We serve him in our neighbor; we see him in the poor; we care for him in the sick; we comfort him in our brothers and sisters who suffer.

If it is authentic, Christian love is transformed immediately into works of service, into a concrete witness given to each person, family, society, and to all of humanity.

Our work is simply an expression of our love of God. We should pour out our love, and others will be the means of expressing our love of God. I think that no one has given more than God, and he has given it all freely. . . . We should constantly thank God for giving us his Son Jesus, for he was born into the world like ourselves, and he was like us in all things except sin. God has manifested the grandeur and beauty of human life by becoming man. (Mother Teresa)

According to Mother Teresa, God's love manifests itself in our suffering neighbor.

We shall be judged according to the way in which we have treated the hungry, the sick, the marginalized. These are our hope and the guaranty of our salvation. We should ap- proach each one of them and treat them as we would treat Christ himself. It does not matter who they are; we must see God in them.

Referring to the witness given by the early Christians, Mother Teresa reflected as follows:

The early Christians lived and died for Jesus, and the people recognized this from the way they loved one another. The world has never needed love as much as today.

We too should be bearers of this love, which bears witness to all!

"All that we do is for Jesus, with Jesus and offered to Jesus."

Poor like Jesus

Poverty has been present throughout all of human history, including our modern times. If we examine the phenomenon of poverty and the natural resources of the earth, we soon come to a dramatic conclusion: Poverty in the world is caused by the selfishness and arrogance of the rich, the exploitation of the poor, and the prevalence of self-interest and injustice.

"On the level of race and social class we find tensions between the affluent and the underdeveloped nations. . . . Great numbers of people are acutely conscious of being deprived of the world's goods through injustice and unfair distribution and are vehemently demanding their share of them. . . . The hungry nations cry out to their affluent neighbors. . . . Now for the first time in history people are not afraid to think that cultural benefits are for all and should be available to everybody" (GS 8-9).

In the face of the dramatic reality which confronts us today, where a few enjoy all the benefits and many others suffer and die or struggle to survive, the problem of poverty is an urgent one. It needs a just and lasting solution if we are to avoid conflicts and wars, and perhaps even the destruction of humanity.

The problem of poverty is a complex one in many respects. Because of the variety of economic, political, cultural, and religious systems, there are also differing concepts of life, family, and society. Then there are differences in climate and environment and in the available technology for exploiting the world's natural resources. This is not to mention the destruction of ecological systems and the autocratic power of multinational corporations.

Moreover, poverty does not only lie in the lack of material goods; more serious and dangerous by far is moral, spiritual and cultural poverty.

What does Jesus teach us about poverty? Does he offer a solution or do we have to be content with the little that we can and ought do for the poor?

Let us look at the life of Jesus. He chose total poverty by becoming incarnate in the womb of the Virgin Mary by the power of the Holy Spirit. "Just as Christ carried out the work of redemption in poverty and oppression, so the Church is called to follow the same path if she is to communicate the fruits of salvation to men. Christ Jesus, 'though he was by nature God . . . emptied himself, taking the nature of a slave' (Ph 2:6, 7) and, 'being rich, became poor' (2 Cor 8:9) for our sake" (LG 8).

"Voluntary poverty, in the footsteps of Christ, is a symbol of Christ which is much esteemed, especially nowadays. Religious should cultivate it diligently and, if need be, express it in new forms" (PC 13).

Jesus was born in extreme poverty, in a cave at Bethlehem, so he could say of himself: "The foxes have lairs, the birds in the sky have nests, but the Son of Man has nowhere to lay his head" (Mt 8:20). He died on the cross, stripped of his clothing, after having been scourged and crucified, and they cast lots for his tunic (cf. Jn 19:23-24). He was buried "in a tomb hewn out

of the rock, in which no one had yet been buried" (Lk 23:53).

Thus, Jesus' life was already an authentic model of poverty. But he went further. He made the way of poverty a condition for salvation. "Do not lay up for yourselves an earthly treasure. Moths and rust corrode; thieves break in and steal. Make it your practice instead to store up heavenly treasure, which neither moths nor rust corrode nor thieves break in and steal. Remember, where your treasure is, there your heart is also" (Mt 6:19-20).

Meditating on this gospel passage, Mother Teresa said:

It would be a shame for us to be wealthier than Jesus. For love of us he subjected himself to poverty. For this reason, our only wealth is Jesus, his love and his presence in our midst.

When he sent the apostles forth to preach, Jesus told them: "Provide yourselves with neither gold nor silver nor copper in your belts; no traveling bag, no change of shirt, no sandals, no walking staff. The workman after all is worth his keep" (Mt 10:9-10).

The apostle's security is Jesus and the message that he bears and preaches to others. For this reason the apostle sets out free of everything and everyone in order to bear witness to Jesus. Thus, poverty becomes freedom; it provides an occasion for loving God and neighbor.

How can we understand the poor if we ourselves do not live poverty? We are poor for the love of Christ; they are constrained by others to be poor. Poverty frees us from things, from everything and everyone in order to belong completely to Jesus. (Mother Teresa)

Commenting on the behavior of the rich young man, who was loved and called by Jesus but refused the invitation because "his possessions were many," Jesus said to his disciples: "I assure you, only with difficulty will a rich man enter into the kingdom of God. I repeat what I said: It is easier for a camel to pass through a needle's eye than for a rich man to enter the kingdom of God" (Mt 19:23-24).

My Congregation must remain faithful to the poor Jesus. We must live with trust in providence. Our greatest danger is to become rich. . . . When my Congregation becomes wealthy, it will die, because we are not simply social workers. The vow of poverty is a great aid in observing chastity and obedience. By our poverty we choose only Jesus; by obedience we listen to him; by chastity we love him. (Mother Teresa)

The freedom that comes from following Jesus alone is expressed this way in the gospel: "None of you can be my disciple if he does not renounce all his possessions" (Lk 14:33).

Poverty is a condition for attaining salvation (cf. Lk 16:19-31). Inspired by Jesus, Mother Teresa has elaborated a personal theology of poverty.

I see Jesus in every person, and especially in the poor and suffering. The poor do not need our help and assistance. . . . They have so little, nothing, but they give so much, everything. . . . Peace will come to the world through the poor because they suffer so much. . . . The poor are our prayer. They carry God within themselves. Jesus said on the cross: "I thirst." It was not a thirst for water but for love. The goal we seek is to placate this thirst. . . . Many people who have much are thirsting for love; they want to be understood and recognized as our brothers and sisters. . . . We want to be totally dependent on the charity of others. We should not be ashamed to go from door to door and beg if it is necessary. . . . At times the Lord suffered real poverty. . . . On the cross he was stripped of everything. The cross itself was given by Pilate. The nails and the crown of thorns were given by the soldiers. He was naked. . . . He was wrapped in a sheet donated by a compassionate bystander and was buried in a tomb that was not his. . . . He chose poverty because he knew that this was the authentic means for possessing God and for bringing God's love down to earth. . . . I believe that people attached to riches, who are preoccupied with wealth, are in reality very poor.

But if they put their money at the service of others, they are rich, very rich. . . . We love and help all the poor, both materially and spiritually, because only in this way can we be faithful to Jesus, loving and helping our neighbor. . . . The poor are marvelous people. They have their dignity, as we can readily verify. . . . For us poverty is love before it is renunciation. To love it is necessary to give. To give it is necessary to be free of selfishness. . . . The heart of the poor opens to us when we can show that we live with them. We must humble ourselves in order to lift them up. (Mother Teresa)

Jesus and the Eucharist

Jesus revealed to his disciples the secrets and treasures of the kingdom of God and of his salvific mission, and he did so gradually. At the outset his words met with misunderstanding, questioning and discussion. And in two instances there was open opposition: at the announcement of his coming death and the promise of the eucharist (cf. Mt 16:21-23; Jn 6:30-70).

"I myself am the bread of life. No one who comes to me shall ever be hungry, no one who believes in me shall ever thirst. . . . I myself am the living bread come down from heaven. If anyone eats this bread he shall live forever; the bread I will give is my flesh, for the life of the world" (Jn 6:35, 51).

The reaction was harsh and derisive: "At this the Jews quarreled among themselves, saying: 'How can he give us his flesh to eat?' Thereupon Jesus said to them: 'Let me solemnly assure you, if you do not eat the flesh of the Son of Man and drink his blood, you have no life in you'" (Jn 6:53).

"At this point his disciples also began to vacillate and many of them murmured: 'This sort of talk is hard to endure! How can anyone take it seriously? . . .' From this time on, many of his disciples broke away and would not remain in his company any longer" (Jn 6:60, 66).

Then Jesus addresses the Twelve and all his followers with sadness but gives them complete freedom: "Do you want to leave me too?" Immediately Peter responds: "Lord, to whom shall we go? You have the words of eternal life. We have come to believe; we are convinced that you are God's holy one" (Jn 6:67-69).

Notice the precision and emphasis of Peter's question: "To whom shall we go?" He does not say: "Where shall we go?" What other relationship could ever replace the one with the holy one of God? When we meditate on the entire chapter 6 of John's gospel, we can conclude:

1) Jesus presents the eucharist as a condition for possessing life. "Let me solemnly assure you, if you do not eat the flesh of the Son of Man and drink his blood, you have no life in you. He who feeds on my flesh and drinks my blood has life eternal, and I will raise him up on the last day" (Jn 6:53-54).

Mother Teresa said:

Our lives must be constantly nourished by the eucharist. Because if we are unable to see Christ under the appearance of bread, neither shall we discover him under the humble appearance of the emaciated bodies of the poor.

2) The eucharist continues and brings to fullness our desire to follow Jesus: "God's bread comes down from heaven and gives life to the world. . . . Indeed, this is the will of my Father, that everyone who looks upon the Son and believes in him shall have eternal life. Him I will raise up on the last day" (Jn 6:33, 40).

One cannot go directly to this friendship meal of the body and blood of Christ without having first "eaten" Jesus with one's eyes, with one's ears, and with one's heart; that is to say, with a living faith and with love.

Faith in act is love, and love in act is service. Jesus said: "I was hungry, I was naked, I was homeless. . . . You have done this to me." We take Christ at his word, and we believe in him. For this reason we have need of the eucharist, because he has become the bread of life to satisfy our desires, our needs, and our love for him. These are the reasons why our life must be closely linked to the eucharist. (Mother Teresa)

3) The eucharist is the beginning of a permanent union with the Master: "The man who feeds on my flesh and drinks my blood remains in me, and I in him" (Jn 6:56).

Eucharistic communion is not a transitory act or moment; much less is it an intermittent devotion. It is the sacrament of a permanent abiding in Jesus, living through him and living with him. "Just as the Father who has life sent me and I have life because of the Father, so the man who feeds on me will have life because of me" (Jn 6:57).

This is also the source of mission.

Jesus became the bread of life so that you and I could eat and live. . . . The meaning of the eucharist is comprehensive love. Jesus understands; he understands that we have a terrible hunger for God. He understood that we were created for love. That is why he became the bread of life. . . . We should eat this bread. The goodness of Christ's love is his comprehensive love. . . . The tabernacle is the proof that he has made his dwelling among us for ever. (Mother Teresa)

4) The eucharist is the seed of the final resurrection. It is also the seed of the glory of our mortal body, a leaven of incorruptibility that transcends death. How often Jesus repeated: "I will raise you up on the last day!" In the eucharist we receive the crucified and risen Christ, and he imprints on us his glorious wounds as a seal of victory over sin, division, death and corruption.

The eucharistic Jesus fosters and increases our union with God and with neighbor. "As often as the sacrifice of the cross by which 'Christ our Pasch is sacrificed' (1 Cor 5:7) is celebrated on the altar, the work of our redemption is carried out. Likewise, in the sacrament of the eucharistic bread, the unity of believers, who form one body in Christ (cf. 1 Cor 10:17), is both expressed and brought about" (LG 3; cf. also 11 and 38).

The Second Vatican Council recommended that "Christ's faithful, when present at this mystery of faith, should not be there as strangers or silent spectators. On the contrary, through a good understanding of the rites and prayers they should take part in the sacred action. . . . They should be instructed by God's word and be nourished at the table of the Lord's body. They should give thanks to God. Offering the immaculate victim, not only through the hands of the priest but also together with him, they should learn to offer themselves. Through Christ, the Mediator, they should be drawn day by day into ever more perfect union with God and each other, so that finally God may be all in all" (SC 48).

"But the other sacraments, and indeed all ecclesiastical ministries and works of the apostolate are bound up with the eucharist and are directed toward it. For in the most blessed eucharist is contained the whole spiritual good of the Church, namely Christ himself, our Pasch and the living bread which gives life to men through his flesh—that flesh which is given life and gives life through the Holy Spirit. Thus men are invited and are led to offer themselves, their works and all creation with Christ" (PO 5).

At this point each of us can and ought to ask: "Is that really the way I live the eucharist?" Why do we unite ourselves to Christ in the eucharist only with our mouth but not with our life, our heart, our entire being? Why do we so quickly forget his presence and return home to resume our life and work as it was? Why do we become preoccupied with so many things that there is either no room left at all for him or at most a small empty corner of our life?

"By the sacraments, and especially by the eucharist, that love of God and man which is the soul of the apostolate is communicated and nourished" (LG 33).

The Way of the Cross: Our Way

*He who will not take up his cross
and come after me is not worthy of me.*
Matthew 10:38

*One cannot follow Christ
without accepting the cross.
Christ is inseparable
from the cross of Calvary. . . .
Those who follow Christ faithfully
are hated by the world,
just as Christ was hated before them,
because they are a challenge
to that type of mentality.*
Mother Teresa

Jesus showed his love for us many times and in various ways. But the culminating manifestation was his suffering, his "way of the cross," his death and resurrection for us and for our salvation. That is why he said: "This is my commandment: love one another as I have loved you. There is no greater love than this: to lay down one's life for one's friends. You are my friends if you do what I command you" (Jn 15:12-14).

Taking upon himself all the world's sins with his precious blood, Jesus has written the most beautiful page in the history of love and sacrifice.

Meditating on the meaning of suffering and the cross, Mother Teresa said:

We should all take up our cross; we should all accompany Jesus in his ascent to Calvary, if we want to arrive with him at the summit of the mountain . . . at the resurrection. The "way of the cross" shows us Jesus, poor and hungry, who falls under the weight of the cross. Are we there to help him? Are we there with our sacrifice, with our piece of bread, with real bread? . . . This is a station of the way of the cross: Jesus is present in those who are hungry and fall beneath the weight of the cross. In the fourth station Jesus meets his mother. Are we mothers to those who suffer? . . . Simon of Cyrene took hold of the cross and walked behind Jesus in order to help him carry it. . . . Veronica; are we like Veronica in relation to the poor? . . . Jesus falls again. How often we have picked up human beings from the street, who were regarded as animals but who accepted death like angels! . . . It is Jesus who needs you to wipe his brow. . . .

He was stripped of his garments. Today, infants are deprived of love even before they are born. They must die, because someone does not want another baby. . . . Jesus is crucified. How many disabled human beings and mentally retarded, many of them in their infancy, fill the hospitals! And how many there are in our families! . . .

Let us begin our way of the cross with courage and joy, because in holy communion we have Jesus with us. . . . Look and you will see that there are persons everywhere who are suffering hunger, and they turn their glance toward us. Do not turn your back on the poor, because the poor are Christ. We should love Christ to the point of sacrifice.

Many people who are suffering feel that they are condemned, abandoned by God and by people; and for that reason they suffer even more, but they suffer badly and to no avail. Mother Teresa had a different experience of suffering, illumined by faith and love:

Suffering is not a punishment. Jesus does not punish. Suffering is a sign—a sign that we are so close to Jesus on the cross that he can kiss us; he can manifest his love by letting us share in his mission to some extent.

"Christ's example in dying for us sinners teaches us that we must carry the cross, which the flesh and the world inflict on the shoulders of all who seek after peace and justice" (GS 38).

The passion of Christ enlightens all suffering; it gives meaning, power and authenticity to all our suffering, both little and great. Only in the light of the cross of Christ do we find an answer to the question why we have to endure so much, why we must carry the cross and at the end die as well.

In his passion our Lord says: "Thy will be done. Do with me what you will." This was all very difficult for our Lord. . . . But he accepted it all in silence, and from the cross he gave us his mother. Then he said: "I thirst" and "It is finished." (Mother Teresa)

From the passion of Christ we also receive this teaching on pardon.

In his passion Jesus has taught us how to forgive out of love, how to forget out of humility. (Mother Teresa)

The cross is the culmination of love and of pardon, the only way to overcome evil, hatred, revenge.

Unfortunately, many persons in our day, including many Christians, accept Christ only partially. They might accept his social teaching, his example of philanthropic love, social justice, or the struggle against national, racial and religious discrimination. But they do not accept Jesus in his suffering, Jesus crucified, dead and risen. Consequently they do not accept his repeated invitation to follow him. This partiality in regard to the person and teaching of Christ empties our faith of content and meaning. As a result, it weakens the plan of our salvation.

Accept everything for Jesus. Accept Jesus, wounded and full of sorrow. . . . Remember that the passion of Christ always ends with the joy of Easter. Don't ever let anything overwhelm you with sorrow to the extent that you forget the joy of the risen Christ. . . . I have thought and meditated so much on the cross. Of itself, suffering is worth nothing; but suffering shared with Christ is a marvelous gift. God loves us precisely through the cross. . . . The Father sent his Son Jesus Christ for the salvation of the world, so that he would die for us and make atonement for our sins, and then rise again for our salvation. Thus, he loves us always. (Mother Teresa)

We can learn a great deal from Jesus' way of the cross:

— Jesus freely and lovingly accepted the cross as an instrument and means for doing his Father's will, for completing the work of salvation.

— His way of the cross is also our way. Like Judas, we sometimes betray him by our sins; at other times, like Peter and the rest of the apostles, we run away out of fear, opportunism or self-interest. Only now and then, perhaps, do we follow him faithfully as did the holy women, together with Mary his mother and John the beloved disciple, or help him carry the cross as did Simon of Cyrene.

— Jesus died for us and for our salvation. As Paul says: "I handed on to you what I myself received, that Christ died for our sins in accordance with the scriptures; that he was buried and, in accordance with the scriptures, rose on the third day; that he was seen by Cephas, then by the Twelve" (1 Cor 15:3-5).

— Jesus brought to completion all the sacrifices of the Old Testament, from the just man Abel to the sacrifice of innocent people in our own day.

— Unless we accept Jesus, live Jesus and love Jesus, and accept his cross as well, we are neither Christians nor his disciples. Without him we cannot overcome evil, sin, the devil or death, nor can we attain salvation. . . .

Jesus, my Lord, my suffering Lord, grant that today and every day I can see you in the person of your sick and grant that also in searching for them I can see you! Let me recognize you in the likeness of the mentally ill so that I can again say to you: My suffering Jesus, how sweet it is to serve you! . . . When we look upon his cross, then we can understand his love: His head is bent to kiss us; his arms are extended to embrace us; his heart is open wide to receive us. (Mother Teresa)

Christ's Resurrection: Our Victory

You will suffer in the world, but take courage! I have overcome the world.
John 16:33

Remember that the passion of Christ always ends in the joy of the resurrection. When you feel in your heart the suffering of Christ, remember that the resurrection will follow, that the joy of Easter will spring forth. Never let yourself be so overcome with sorrow that you forget the joy of the risen Christ.
Mother Teresa

After the death of Christ the apostles felt abandoned and hopeless. Their sorrow was so intense that they were unable to understand anything that had happened. It seemed like the end of the world. One of them, Judas, no longer had the courage to go on living or to ask pardon for what he had done. The rest of the apostles went into hiding for fear of the Jews. Some of the disciples, like the two on the road to Emmaus, were now returning to their homes, disappointed, discouraged and depressed. They may have been thinking that their association with Jesus had been quite an adventure, but it was too beautiful to be true or to last. It was all over now, and it had ended badly!

Good Friday seemed as long as an eternity! If asked, many would have said that perhaps it all had to end that way; that Jesus had deceived himself and others as well. Crowds of people were in Jerusalem for the feast days, enjoying themselves. But the apostles were sad and lonely, waiting to see what would happen next.

The enemies of Jesus were satisfied and happy. Very likely they were thinking: "We have finally eliminated the one who was attacking us in public, performing miracles, and teaching a new doctrine to the people." At last they were able to enjoy the feast day with the people in peace!

The contrast is great. But Jesus' friends did

not give up completely. They could recall that Jesus had frequently surprised them by showing that he is master over death. He resurrected Lazarus (Jn 11:1-44), the daughter of the synagogue leader (Mt 9:18-26), the son of the widow of Naim (Lk 7:11-17), and he had performed numerous miracles and extraordinary feats. "Perhaps there is something behind his own death that we have not understood."

The apostles, a few women and some selected witnesses have now verified that Jesus is no longer dead; he is risen. They have seen him alive; they have spoken with him; they have touched him. He is alive!

"On the evening of that first day of the week, even though the disciples had locked the doors of the place where they were for fear of the Jews, Jesus came and stood before them. 'Peace be with you,' he said. When he had said this, he showed them his hands and his side. At the sight of the Lord the disciples rejoiced" (Jn 20:19-20).

But Thomas, one of the Twelve, was doubtful. "His answer was, 'I will never believe it without probing the nailprints in his hands, without putting my finger in the nailmarks and my hand into his side.' A week later the disciples were once more in the room, and this time Thomas was with them. Despite the locked doors, Jesus came and stood before them. 'Peace be with you,' he said; then, to Thomas: 'Take your finger and examine my hands. Put your hand into my side. Do not persist in your unbelief, but believe!' Thomas said in response, 'My Lord and my God!' Jesus then said to him: 'You became a believer because you saw me. Blest are they who have not seen and have believed'" (Jn 20:24-29).

Jesus also appeared to some of the women (Lk 24:1-12), to the disciples on the road to Emmaus (Lk 24:13-35), and to the apostles (Mt 28:16-20; Mk 16:14-18; Jn 20:19-23; Acts 1:6-8; 2:24; 3:15; 4:10, 33; 5:30; 10:40; 13:30).

With the resurrection of Jesus, everything was changed: night into day, sadness into joy, doubt into certitude, death into life.

"In the human nature united to himself, the Son of God, by overcoming death through his own death and resurrection, redeemed man and changed him into a new creation" (LG 7; cf. GS 39).

It is likewise from the resurrection of Jesus that a dramatic change took place in the apostles. Now they courageously announced the good news to the people: Jesus is alive! He is risen! He has overcome death and the world!

The news quickly spread everywhere throughout Jerusalem. The apostles no longer had any doubts, questions or fears. They began to preach the resurrection of Christ before the authorities and the people (cf. Acts 2:22-24, 36). Later on, they gave witness by their sufferings (Acts 4:10-12) and even more so by their martyrdom.

The keystone of our faith is precisely the resurrection of Christ. It is the inexhaustible font of life, of pardon, of love and of salvation. . . .

May the joy of the risen Christ be with you. . . . Easter is the greatest feast in our Congregation. . . . It gives witness to the new life in Christ that has been given us. (Mother Teresa)

The Church in Albania has lived a traumatic situation for years. Under atheistic dictatorship, the country would not even give Mother

Teresa permission to visit her mother, Drane Bojaxhiu and her sister, Age Bojaxhiu. She bore this immense suffering with great faith, saying:

Now I am able to obtain everything through love and prayer. There are still some obstacles that even love cannot overcome. . . . I do not know exactly what is happening in Albania, but I know that I always pray to the good God for them and I am convinced that through prayer he will bestow many graces on them. . . . I think that our Church in Albania has not yet passed through its Good Friday, but our faith tells us that the life of Jesus did not end that way. It went on to the cross and terminated in the resurrection. My Albanian people cannot and should not forget this.

On another occasion she stated:

Here is the secret of Christian success. Christ gave his life so that it could become our life, present in every individual, in every family.

The Second Vatican Council stated: "The Christian is certainly bound both by need and by duty to struggle with evil through many afflictions and to suffer death; but, as one who has been made a partner in the paschal mystery, and as one who has been configured to the death of Christ, he will go forward, strengthened by hope, to the resurrection. . . . For since Christ died for all, and since all men are in fact called to one and the same destiny, which is divine, we must hold that the Holy Spirit offers to all the possibility of being made partners . . . in the paschal mystery" (GS 22).

The focal point of the week is Sunday, the Lord's Day, when the Church "keeps the memory of the Lord's resurrection. She also celebrates it once every year, together with his blessed passion, at Easter, that most solemn of all feasts" (SC 102; cf. 106).

The resurrection of Christ is the fundamental truth of our faith because it opens up immense possibilities for our daily Christian activity. It gives us the certitude of salvation, and it opens to us the horizon of eternity.

"If Christ has not been raised, our preaching is void of content, and your faith is empty too. . . . If Christ was not raised, your faith is worthless. You are still in your sins. . . . If our hopes in Christ are limited to this life only, we are the most pitiable of men" (1 Cor 15:14-19).

The guaranty of our salvation and immortality has been written with the precious blood of Christ and sealed with his resurrection. It is precisely for this reason that we can believe, proclaim and give witness to the world: The resurrection of Christ is our victory!

Jesus Still Lives Today

And know that I am with you always,
until the end of the world!
Matthew 28:20

We should let the good God
carry out every project in the future,
for yesterday is gone,
tomorrow has not yet arrived,
and we have only today
to make him known, loved and served.
Mother Teresa

During his life on earth Jesus met many different kinds of people in various circumstances. Moreover, he came in contact with suffering, sin, and death; in a word, with all the complexities of human existence.

Many people listened to him, but few really understood him.

Many sought after him, but few really found him.

Many were attracted by his words and actions, but very few were courageous enough to leave all things and follow him.

Many marveled at him, but few discovered the real significance of his miracles.

Many needed him, but only for some of them did he perform miracles, publicly forgive their sins or deliver them from slavery to the devil.

Many followed him, but only a few were chosen and called: the apostles and disciples.

Similarly today:

Many persons say that they believe, but perhaps few consistently live their faith and the gospel.

Many people pray, but perhaps few really converse with God and their neighbor.

Many receive the sacraments, but perhaps only some or a few of them are truly united to Jesus and live with him.

Many seek him, but few find him. Why?

As it was then, so it is today. Only those who seek him with faith and love, with a pure and sincere heart, can find and live Jesus. As Mother Teresa stated:

Only the one who prays and loves with a pure heart can find God.

To find Jesus today, it is necessary first of all:

— to recognize and find him in the Bible, especially in the New Testament, and more importantly still, in the gospels, which are his words of life. "Thus, as the centuries go by, the Church is always advancing toward the plenitude of divine truth, until eventually the words of God are fulfilled in her" (DV 8; cf. also 14-21);

— to recognize his presence and vitality in the Church and especially in the sacraments, in the eucharist in particular;

— to find him in our neighbor, in every person, and in the circumstances of life.

It is necessary to acknowledge our sins and our limitations, but even more than that, the goodness, mercy and pardon of God. We need to have great faith, hope and love, "because love is of God; everyone who loves is begotten of God and has knowledge of God. The man without love has known nothing of God, for God is love" (1 Jn 4:7-8).

Jesus still lives today and is present in the Church, which continues his work "to bring salvation to all" (IM 3). Jesus "founded his Church as the sacrament of salvation; and just as he had been sent by the Father (cf. Jn 20:21), so he sent the apostles into the whole world" (AG 5; cf. GS 44).

The Church helps us to be united with God and neighbor, because it is "at once manifesting and actualizing the mystery of God's love" for us (GS 45).

The Church gathers together all people on earth into a new people: God "willed to make men holy and save them, not as individuals without any bond or link between them, but rather to make them into a people who might acknowledge him and serve him in holiness. . . . Christ instituted this new covenant, namely the new covenant in his blood (cf. 1 Cor 11:25); he called a race, made up of Jews and Gentiles, which would be one, not according to the flesh, but in the Spirit, and this race would be the new people of God" (LG 9).

Christ's presence in the Church is actualized especially in the liturgy: "To accomplish so great a work Christ is always present in his Church, especially in her liturgical celebrations. He is present in the sacrifice of the Mass not only in the person of his minister . . . but especially in the eucharistic species. By his power he is present in the sacraments" (SC 7).

Every human being, every epoch, culture, and race has need of God. This is true today more than ever, even if this need is not recognized or clearly stated.

I think that people today have a much greater hunger for God than in any previous time. There is a hunger for ordinary bread and a hunger for love, for goodness and care. The young especially have an infinite hunger and thirst. But very often they are unable to see God in us. And this is something that young people cannot accept. We say one thing, but we do another. This keeps them at a distance from us and is the fundamental reason for the lack of many vocations and the destruction of others. . . . Young people today don't want to listen; they want to see. . . . We talk a great deal about God, but perhaps we live him very little. (Mother Teresa)

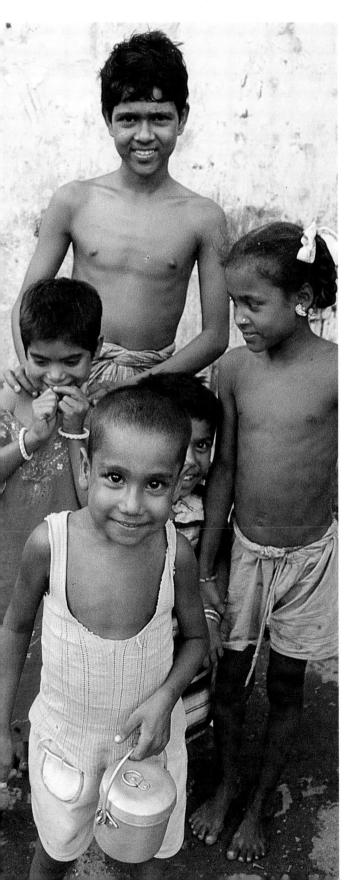

To know and to live God today, the Church needs many authentic witnesses of Christ's presence.

It is necessary to live the gospel and bear witness about it to others; to listen to the word of God in the very depths of our being and with a pure heart. Before proclaiming it, you must listen, because God speaks in the silence of your heart. . . . Today, once again, when Jesus comes among us, his own do not know him.

He comes in the repugnant bodies of the poor, but he comes also in the rich, who are suffocated by their wealth.

He comes in the loneliness of their hearts, and when there is no one to love them.

Jesus also comes to you and to me, but frequently, very frequently, we pass him by. (Mother Teresa)

Jesus still lives today. He is present to us in so many ways. But are we capable, or better yet, are we ready to recognize him, love him, and give witness of him to others? The answer to this question lies in our lifestyle:

Jesus offers to all the souls who seek him a face-to-face encounter, to accept him or reject him. . . . I would be ready to give up my life, but not my faith. . . . Faith is lacking in the world today because there is too much self-ishness and too much striving for financial gain. . . . Love and faith walk side by side . . . they perfect each other. Consequently, if faith is to be authentic, there must be a love that gives. (Mother Teresa)

Who Is Jesus for Us?

"You are the Messiah,"
Simon Peter answered,
"the Son of the living God!"
Matthew 16:16

My greatest reward is to love Jesus.
He is everything to me.
He is my life, my love,
my recompense, my all.
Mother Teresa

The most important question of our life, the one on which eternity and everything else depends, is precisely this: "Who is Jesus for me, for us?"

It is an inevitable question for everyone. Even more so for the Christian who wants not only an intellectual response that can be found by anyone, but a personal answer that is dynamic and existential. We need to examine our life to live more fully.

This same question was asked by the apostles and has been repeated in every age during two thousand years of Christianity. In order to answer it, we follow the methodology used by Jesus. He himself asked his disciples: "Who do people say that the Son of Man is?" (Mt 6:13).

As was the case then, also today there are many answers and opinions concerning Jesus. Some people were expecting that Jesus would liberate the Chosen People from their political, economic and social subservience to the Romans. Consequently, they were disappointed with Jesus. Others rejected him because he was too demanding; he insisted on conversion and a complete change of life. But there were others who accepted him: the apostles, his disciples and friends among which there were women and children, as well as sinners, the poor and the sick. Finally, there were also those who were openly opposed to Jesus and tried in every way possible to do away with him.

Likewise today, Jesus' question receives many different answers. What do people today say of Jesus? of the Church and Christianity? of the life of our parish community, knowing us as disciples of Christ?

The second part of the question posed by Jesus is this: "'And you,' he said to them, 'who do you say that I am'" (Mt 16:15).

Once again, Simon Peter answers in the name of all the apostles: "You are the Messiah . . . the Son of the living God!" (Mt 16:16). This is the marvelous confession of Peter, of the apostles, and of all those who believe in Jesus.

Christ praised Peter for his response: "Blest are you, Simon, son of John! No mere man has revealed this to you, but my heavenly Father" (Mt 16:17).

Commenting on this passage of scripture, Mother Teresa wrote:

You are God.
You are true God from true God.
Generated not created.
Of the selfsame substance of the Father.
You are the Second Person of the most
   holy Trinity.
You are one in being with the Father.
You are with the Father from all eternity.
All things were created by you and the Father.
You are the Beloved Son in whom the Father
   is well pleased.
You are the Son of Mary, conceived by
the Holy Spirit in her virginal womb.
You were born in Bethlehem.
You were wrapped in swaddling clothes
   by Mary

and placed in a manger filled with straw.
You are an ordinary man without much
education, and the educated class in Israel
judges you.
Jesus is: the Word made flesh . . .
the bread of life,
the victim immolated for our sins on the cross,
the sacrifice offered for the sins of the world
and for my sins in the Holy Mass,
the word to be proclaimed,
the truth to be revealed,
the way to be followed,
the light to illumine,
the life to live,
the love to be loved,
the hungry person to be fed,
the thirsty person given drink,
the naked one to clothe,
the homeless to receive shelter,
the sick to be cured,
the abandoned to be loved,
the outcast to be welcomed,
the leper whose wounds are bathed,
the beggar to whom a smile is given,
the drunkard who needs to be listened to,
the mentally disturbed who needs to be
   protected,
the infant who needs to be held in our arms,
the blind person who needs to be led by the
   hand,
the mute for whom someone must speak,
the crippled with whom one walks,
the drug addict who needs help,
the prostitute who needs to be taken
off the street and listened to,
the prisoner who needs to be visited,
the aged person who needs to be taken
   care of.

I once asked Mother Teresa to explain to me the secret of a life lived so intensely for God, for the Church, and for every suffering human being. She responded cordially and simply:

My secret is Jesus and his great love for us, prayer and meditation, the daily hour of adoration, our religious vows. My motto is: Everything for Jesus; all for Jesus through Mary. Look at the five fingers of my hand. He has made all this for me! Remember to look at your hand and your five fingers, every morning and night, and during the examination of conscience. What have I done for Jesus?

But let us return to our earlier question: "What do people think of Jesus today?"

What do we say to the world and what kind of witness do we give as to who Jesus is?

Our very life and salvation depend on this question. It is better to face it now, because tomorrow it may be too difficult or too late!

The world expects from us a coherent, clear, courageous and sincere answer; one that will arouse in others a desire to be like us and, even better, like Jesus! This kind of answer can be given only by our life, our faith and our love!

Mother Teresa advises:

We do not try to impose our faith on others. We try to act in such a way that Christ will make his light and his life shine forth in us and, through us, in the world.

To Admire or to Follow Jesus

Jesus has been and is a historical, religious, cultural and moral phenomenon. No one can be indifferent to him; his personality and figure demand of us a fundamental choice: to be with him or against him.

During his life on earth, Jesus aroused the admiration of many, especially through his miracles. For example, when he raised the daughter of Jairus (Mk 5:21-43), the young man of Naim (Lk 7:11-17), his friend Lazarus (Jn 11:1-48), when he calmed the storm (Mt 6:23-27) and cured the paralytic (Mt 9:1-8).

"In this fashion the crowd was sharply divided over him. Some of them even wanted to apprehend him. However, no one laid hands on him" (Jn 7:43-44).

The chief priests and Pharisees were disturbed and agitated. They were uncertain what to do about Jesus, because he had been well received by the people. He was admired and loved and even followed by many. Finally they decided to command the guards to seize him. His enemies remained fearful as they awaited the outcome of their actions.

How surprised they were when the guards returned without Jesus! They asked: "Why did you not bring him in?" The guards replied: "No man ever spoke like that before" (Jn 7:45-46).

Such is the testimony of the guards. They are enthusiastic about Jesus but don't go further.

They simply report the facts. They are happy to have found him, to have listened to him and known him. But that is all.

But this attitude causes even greater confusion for Jesus' enemies. The Pharisees reply: "Do not tell us you too have been taken in!" (Jn 7:47).

Instead of considering the testimony of the guards, the enemies simply grow in hatred and disdain for Jesus and for the guards as well. "You do not see any of the Sanhedrin believing in him, do you? Or the Pharisees? Only this lot, that knows nothing about the law—and they are lost anyway!" (Jn 7:48-49). The Pharisees seem to consider themselves to be the only just and chosen ones and despise everyone else!

The testimony of the guards is valuable and sincere. Although they had been sent to apprehend him, they had the courage to listen to Jesus, to look at him and admire him! But according to those who had sent the guards, Jesus was a deceiver, an agitator, an enemy of God and of the people.

We must see, hear and judge others on the basis of what they really are, without prejudice. We should recognize and acknowledge whatever degree of goodness there is in others, even in our enemies. Other persons are not like ourselves; they do not think or speak or believe as we do! . . .

In a way the guards resemble the world of today, with its social and cultural roots in Christianity. Christ and the gospel have inspired creativity for many centuries and still do today. As did the Jewish guards, many say today that Jesus is remarkable, unique, humble, friendly, generous and good. Even those who do not believe in him admit this much.

Gandhi once said that if Christians were truly such, there would be no Hindus in India. Everyone expects of us that we should live our Christian life to the full. (Mother Teresa)

If this is how Jesus is, what should we, his disciples, be? What should our Church and society be after two thousand years? Jesus is not merely teaching an idea or an ideology. He is the Word of God made flesh, a reality, man. We can meet him, love him, and give witness to him. He is love, who offers himself and awaits our response.

Perhaps many people know the message of Jesus well enough; they write and speak about him. But what good is this if they do not live him? People are tired of work, tired of life. They read very little and they read badly, but they "read" our life as Christians very attentively.

The Christian is the tabernacle of the living God. (Mother Teresa)

To know Jesus without living and giving witness to him is useless, because then Jesus remains only an idea or ideology but not the fullness of life that he really is (cf. Jn 1:1-4).

To admire Jesus is something very beautiful, but it is too little, scarcely the first step. To love him, live him, follow him and bear witness to him, this is our calling and our life.

We should not be afraid to proclaim the love of Christ, and to love as he loved. Put the love of Christ in the work that you must do, however little or humble it is. . . . People do not admire our work or our professionalism but our faith, our love of Jesus, our love for the poor and for every human being. . . . Let us help people to discover, know, love and serve Jesus in the suffering. (Mother Teresa)

Also in the world today there are many who sympathize with Christ. "Since Christians have different gifts, they should collaborate in the work of the gospel, each according to his opportunity, ability, charism and ministry" (AG 28).

Every Christian is called not only to admire but to follow, live and give witness to Jesus.

**Mother Teresa and Chiara Lubich
at the Extraordinary Synod of Bishops in 1985**

To Witness

Happiness

I assure you,
as often as you did it
for one of my least brothers,
you did it for me.
Matthew 25:40

Joy is a necessity,
a great gift for others
and also for ourselves.
It is the flame of an ardent love.
Joy is prayer; joy is power;
joy is love in action.
Mother Teresa

The desire and need for happiness is fundamental; it is common to all human beings. People express this desire in many different ways, some of them as ordinary as Merry Christmas, Happy New Year, Happy Birthday, Happy Feast Day. At other times, when we don't have words especially suited for the occasion, we may simply say Have a nice day! or Good Luck! or something similar. On more solemn and formal occasions we choose expressions that fit the occasion, but they will always have as a central theme the desire for happiness, success, good fortune, joy or love.

Everyone wants to be happy and successful. Many go as far as to consult the horoscope to find out what their future holds. But one cannot buy or sell happiness. That is why it is better to be happy than it is to be rich. Without happiness one loses the joy of living.

If happiness is so important to everyone, we need to ask a practical question: What must one do to be happy? And even more fundamentally: What is happiness? How can one achieve it and preserve it for as long as possible? Even when we are happy and tranquil in the midst of friends and acquaintances, full of life and love, the thought comes to mind: How long will this last? What will our life be like tomorrow?

One thing is certain: We cannot be happy if we are closed within ourselves; much less if we seek to avoid others or ourselves. Consequently, we need to reflect on some basic questions:

— Who am I as an individual within my social, religious, national and cultural context?

—What do I expect from life, from my work, from others or from myself?

—What do I expect from God, from my faith and from the Church?

—What do others mean to me, and what do they expect from me?

In our life and work we need to maintain the proper balance between self and others and between self and God. If we do not achieve the necessary harmony and dialogue in these relationships, we fail and happiness vanishes, frequently at the expense of others. To separate oneself from others, who are also seeking happiness and love, is futile. Life teaches us that we can be happy only in relationship with others, only when we live and sacrifice ourselves for others, and when they do the same for us.

Unfortunately, egoism is often strong and overbearing. When we strive at any cost to impose ourselves, essentially using others to achieve our own happiness, we harm them and ourselves. In this case we invest much, even our whole life, in the futile search for self-satisfaction. As a result, we enjoy only a partial and fleeting happiness, which later leaves us dissatisfied and empty. Those who seek only themselves find neither themselves nor others. If they do live with others, they only use them. Deluded and mistaken, they are enslaved to small pleasures and successes, full of self but at the same time empty. As a result, life becomes an exhausting process of disintegration.

Such a self-centered life has serious repercussions in the spiritual and religious life. We end up living a God-centered life only from time to time,

in special moments and circumstances. This discontinuity creates uncertainty and instability. Life then becomes a game of chance, dependent on circumstances, events, individuals. No longer do we live life; we simply endure it and in so doing risk a great deal, in fact, everything.

Many people, even after so many failures, so many false and empty choices, nevertheless continue on the same tortuous path. They have no idea where they are, what they want, or where they are going. Then they constantly ask themselves: Why am I so unhappy? Is it because other people are inhuman and unjust? Because they tread on me, reject me and hate me? Why is it that even God treats me unfairly?

The answer is quite simple. From the moment that an individual seeks only oneself, rather than others or the Other who is God, he or she will be a prisoner in the closed circle of egoism and unhappiness.

Happiness is a process. It involves the development of life, love, sacrifice and altruism. It is based on a life directed toward God and neighbor. True happiness consists in knowing, loving and doing God's will, living in harmony with God and neighbor or, as we would put it today, in being a man or woman of God, a true human being living among and for others.

If we would aim our energies in this direction, we would be much more secure, even in moments of failure and unhappiness. Our daily lives might still be a mixture of light and shadow, but at the same time they would be filled with love, sacrifice and happiness.

True happiness consists of suffering endured with love and in love, of traveling along the secure but arduous path toward the proper goal. It means to trustfully abandon ourselves into the hands of God our Father and into the embrace of our brothers and sisters. To accept oneself with one's limitations and dependencies, with one's own past, present and future, means to entrust oneself definitively to God. It implies to accept the role or position that he has decreed for us in the plan of salvation. Jesus expressed this by saying, "Whoever does not accept the kingdom of God as a child will not enter into it" (Lk 18:17). This is what constitutes maturity in the faith and in religious life.

To accept others is to love them, respect them, collaborate with them. It means to live with them and for them, no longer out of self-interest, but realizing that others were also created by God out of love and for love! This understanding provides a basis for being brothers and sisters in the faith, for empathy, understanding, trust, solidarity and sharing. This is what teaches a person how to give and receive, even to the point of sacrificing oneself for others.

Seen with the eyes of faith, the other is not only a creature of God, a child of God, and our brother or sister, but something more. He or she is Jesus Christ for us, in accordance with his teaching: "As often as you did it for one of my least brothers, you did it for me" (Mt 25:40).

Ultimately, others are for us the presence of the Lord, who comes to us asking for practical, faithful, and true love. But first he offers to us his great love and our salvation. This is what constitutes true Christian joy. It is the inexhaustible font of our happiness on earth and in eternity.

Joy is a net of love with which we can fish for souls. God loves a joyful giver. The best way of showing our gratitude to God and neighbor is to receive them with love. . . . To be happy in God means to love as he does, to help as he does, to give as he does, and to serve as he does. . . . In your traveling to and fro, spread around you the joy of belonging to God, of living with God, of being with God, of loving God in your neighbor. . . . To be happy and to spread joy costs very little. Each day try to do God's will, because the world hungers for God and for his love. Pray always; know how to love and to pardon. Impatiently we await paradise, where God is, but it is within our power to be in paradise even now, from the very moment that we love and sacrifice ourselves for God and for our suffering neighbor. (Mother Teresa)

"The Word of God, through whom all things were made, was made flesh, so that as a perfect man he could save all men and sum up all things in himself. The Lord is the goal of human history, the focal point of the desires of history and civilization, the center of mankind, the joy of all hearts, and the fulfillment of all aspirations" (GS 45).

Happiness is a need for every human being. Let us try to be happy, to know what constitutes true happiness, to make others happy too by letting them share in our happiness. It is beautiful and precious to live and to love that way. To work that way is beneficial to all.

It costs us so little to be happy and to make other people happy: a hand extended in friendship, a cordial greeting, a friendly smile.

The world today is hungering for the joy that comes from a pure heart, because the pure of heart see God. . . . A smile costs little but it does so much good. . . . Joy shines forth in the eyes and in the glance, in one's conversation and in the expression of one's countenance. When people see the happiness in your eyes, they will discover God within you. (Mother Teresa)

Return to the Sources

*Rising early the next morning,
he went off to a lonely place in the desert;
there he was absorbed in prayer.*
Mark 1:35

*To work or live without love is a form of
slavery. The Church wants a renewal of
herself in the world of today.
But a renewal is not simply a change of
clothing, something purely external;
it is primarily an interior, radical change
of the human heart by the grace of God.*
Mother Teresa

Every work or activity should be an expression of ourselves, prompted by a spirit of love and service. The gospel tells us: "If one of you decides to build a tower, will he not first sit down and calculate the outlay to see if he has enough money to complete the project? He will do that for fear of laying the foundation and then not being able to complete the work; for all who saw it would jeer at him, saying, 'That man began to build what he could not finish'" (Lk 14:28-30).

The uncertainty and preoccupation of life together with the toil, pain and fatigue of work often cause us to feel like strangers to ourselves and to others. This results in a behavior based on our need to be like everybody else, not differing from others either in good or in evil.

To live our life this way, without any goal and choice, is like driving a car without brakes, a ship without a rudder, or driving while drunk. It is dangerous for us and for others, like trying to keep our balance when walking on ice.

To live without prayer, without the spiritual power that comes from meditation and interior silence, could eventually lead to a burdensome, sad and uncertain existence.

Prayer is not a flight from one's daily active life; much less is it a flight from oneself, from others and from the world. It is a very authen-

tic search for the true face of others and of God under the impetus of love and faith, which enables us to discover, understand and more readily accept who we are, who others are, who God is, and what the meaning is of our life and work, and all that we are and do. (Mother Teresa)

Unfortunately, people today, many believers included, no longer know how to pray. They are almost completely absorbed in external matters, in the world that surrounds them, absorbs their attention, drains and dominates them, and ultimately seriously harms them. The interior life becomes a market place for buying and selling, as the gospel describes it. No longer is it a temple, a place of silence and prayer, where we meet the living God. The temple is thus profaned, causing a vehement reaction from Jesus: "Jesus entered the temple precincts and drove out all those engaged there in buying and selling. He overturned the money changers' tables and the stalls of the dove-sellers, saying to them, 'Scripture has it, "My house shall be called a house of prayer," but you are turning it into a den of thieves'" (Mt 21:12-13).

Let us invite Jesus also into the temple of our heart, into the intimacy of our interior life. May he put it in order, driving out whatever oppresses us, profanes us, drains and harms us. Only through him can we do it.

To concentrate on the external life alone, without interior peace and tranquillity, which are the heritage of the spirit, turns us into slaves. It exhausts us by removing something day by day that is an essential part of our nature.

People today are busy almost every day of the week, burdened with professional duties to earn a livelihood, with social and community obligations, working for financial gain or for personal success. Many people can escape the daily routine only on weekends or during vacation. There they will seek out moments of quiet and relaxation, maybe in the tranquillity and beauty of nature, to be able later to return to the noise, distraction and tension of daily stressful duties.

During these flights from the monotony of daily tasks there is also the danger of fleeing from oneself, from others or from God. Relatively few people today have the strength—and the courage—to stop and ask themselves where they are going, what they are seeking and who they are. Instead, the frenzied pace continues, and we no longer recognize ourselves.

We have become aware for some time now that we have been distancing ourselves farther and farther from nature. That is why so many today are supporting various ecology projects. But there is also a need for spiritual ecology, due to the desert of moral, religious and cultural values that surrounds us. The situation gives reason enough to worry. We are destroying everything imaginable. Our motto seems to be "Live for today!" as we enjoy every pleasure, thinking only of our unlimited personal gain. Surrounded by the wasteland of a consumer society, we spend lavishly to possess and use everything, only to then discard it. We are hemmed in by the circle of labor and production; everything is weighed on the materialistic and economic scale.

To return to our roots means returning to ourselves, to others and especially to God, the only source of peace, security, love, and happiness. To be constantly busy, working day and night to live more comfortably, may very well conceal an even more dangerous tendency: the dread of facing ourselves, the inability to relate to others, the fear of God. Activism then becomes a continuous flight that can lead to serious consequences. We work, produce, make money, enjoy life to such an extent that we lose our sense of balance. The result is a person so self-centered and aloof from others that his or her heart has turned cold.

We all gradually accumulate numerous experiences. Many things happen inside ourselves and around us, and sometimes we do not even have the time to react to them, to put them in order and digest them. This situation can lead to great stress and destroy our rapport with others and with the world around us. Without a good balance between action and contemplation, we cannot be secure and happy with our life and work. Our Christian mission in the world of today is this: to cultivate a dynamic rapport between ourselves and others and God. Only then shall we be able to live, to learn and to communicate with others.

Throughout the whole world there is a terrible longing, a terrible hunger for love, for God. There can be no interior life, no communion among brothers and sisters, without the practice of prayer. To be fruitful, prayer must come from the heart and be capable to touch the heart of God. See how Jesus taught his disciples to pray. Call God your Father; praise and glorify his name. Often our prayers, like everything else in our lives, are superficial. We have not fastened our mind and heart to Jesus, through whom our prayers can rise to God. Sometimes a fervent glance at Jesus can make our prayer more fervent. I look at him, and he looks at me; that is a perfect prayer. . . . My work does not

distract me from God. When the Sisters travel around, the poor do not ask them for clothing or for something to eat. They only say: "Teach us the word of God. . . ." I have often thought that it would be nice to go off and live with the contemplative Sisters, to live a life that is totally separated from the world, to simply be with Jesus. But then I realized that I can be like that even when traveling around the world, working and praying. Now I am the happiest person in the world, because I am living with Jesus twenty-four hours a day. . . . As to the poor of the world, I would say that they all want to feel that they have a Father in heaven, a Father who loves them. (Mother Teresa)

This, then, is what it means to return to the sources: to return to living not only by "Our Father in heaven," but also by "Our Father here below on earth"; to live as brothers and sisters under the love of our common Father. We must return constantly to the inexhaustible source of life and love—to God—through others, while being within ourselves what God wants us to be.

"The Spirit dwells in the Church and in the hearts of the faithful as in a temple. In them he prays and bears witness to their adoptive sonship. Guiding the Church in the way of all truth and unifying her in communion and in the works of ministry, he bestows upon her varied hierarchic and charismatic gifts, and in this way directs her; and he adorns her with his fruits. By the power of the gospel he permits the Church to keep the freshness of youth. Constantly he renews her and leads her to perfect union with her Spouse. . . . Hence the universal Church is seen to be 'a people brought into unity from the unity of the Father, the Son and the Holy Spirit'" (LG 4).

The Voice of Silence

We live in a world full of sounds, signals, images, computerized communication, both international and even extraterrestrial. We have reached fantastic limits in scientific achievement; we are understanding and conquering the universe. The technology of communication has made giant strides that amaze everyone. As a result, the world today is getting smaller and smaller, while humanity looms ever larger as the conqueror of space and time.

Nevertheless, we are who we are, with our limitations and defects, with our great and small problems, with countless possibilities as well as joys and sorrows. We are constantly searching for the meaning of all that happens within and around us.

The progress of the world in communications has greatly facilitated advances in knowledge, information, culture and techniques. But unfortunately it has not greatly helped humanity to become more human, friendly, and sociable. Instead, the contrary has happened. While communication in space is becoming ever more easy and common, within our families and toward our neighbors we are increasingly solitary and distant strangers, locked up within ourselves. We resemble a mysterious fortress, isolated and empty, and surrounded by social disinterest. Our interpersonal relationships are full of information, but at the same time we are deaf, mute, blind, satiated and weary.

The greatest challenge, and perhaps the decisive one in the struggle for humanity's recovery, is the restoration of fundamental values, without which we remain in a dark and uncertain void, building castles in the air. And it is precisely for this reason that we have such a need for silence; not passive silence, but the voice of silence, the language of a deep interior life, the search for self, for others, and especially for the Creator and his message of love and pardon.

For so many people today, silence seems to be impossible to attain. They see it as a waste of time and avoid at any cost the encounter with self. Here is where the techniques of escape come into play. People are bombarded from all sides by sounds, images and noise of every kind, preventing them from thinking, from being alone, from hearing the voice of silence and of their conscience, which is louder than any other voice.

As believers and Christians, we have instead a positive concept of silence, because in it we can hear ourselves and be ourselves. In silent recollection and prayer, we can hear God's voice within us, as long as our antennae are turned toward God, who wants to be in constant communication with us.

A true interior life makes the active life burn with fervor and consume everything. This enables us to meet God in the darkest corners of the slums, in the saddest misery of the poor. It puts us in contact with the naked God-man on the cross; sad, despised by all, a man of sorrows, disdained like a worm. . . . And it is precisely because of this that we have such a great need for silence; the silence of humility, of charity; silence of the eyes and ears and tongue. Without this, the life of prayer does not exist. Silence leads to charity, and charity to humility. God speaks to us in silence, in prayer, in adoration, in the interior life. For that reason I insist on recommending silence. Silence of the tongue teaches us to speak of Christ and makes it possible for Christ to speak to us. Silence of the eyes enables us to see God. Our eyes are like two windows through which Christ can enter the world.

Sometimes we must have the courage to remain closed. We observe the silence of the heart, like the Blessed Virgin, who kept everything in her heart. Prayerful souls are souls of great silence. We cannot place ourselves in the presence of God without committing ourselves to interior and exterior silence. God is a friend of silence; he speaks to us in silence. We must find God, but God cannot be found in noise, distractions or agitation. . . . If we are not able to accept ourselves and others, how can we communicate with God? The more we receive from our silent prayer, the more we can give in our active life. Silence gives us a clear vision of things. . . . The essential thing is not what we say, but what God says to us, and to others through us. Jesus waits for us in the silence of the tabernacle; he listens to us and he speaks to us; he loves us and makes us capable of loving him and of bearing witness of him to the world. (Mother Teresa)

Silence is the X-ray of our life; it helps us to know ourselves, to gain energy for improvement, and to be available to God and neighbor.

The voice of silence, then, is the prayer of the heart, in-depth meditation, time reserved for communicating with God. It will help us to become better and to integrate the various parts of our life, to examine and evaluate, and—why not?—to correct and change our life, together with Jesus our Master.

From this are born and developed great works of God, with our cooperation, for the service of all. One who is filled with God does not live all alone in silence and prayer, but must live-act-witness everywhere to love and to life: to God. Such a person is continually and intimately bound to God and consequently also to humanity.

Silence, prayer, meditation, the sacramental life: These prepare for great works in the world. A clear and evident proof of this is Mother Teresa. She was a living witness of this reality. Behold this light or city set upon a hill, which cannot be hidden (cf. Mt 5:14).

It Is Possible to Live the Gospel

*"To other towns I must announce
the good news of the reign of God,
because that is why I was sent."
And he continued to preach
in the synagogues of Judea.*
Luke 4:43-44

*For me the gospel is the word of life;
it is Jesus who speaks to us
and teaches us today in the Church
and through the Church.*
Mother Teresa

Jesus Christ and Christianity are an integral part of our tradition, culture and, to some extent, worldwide civilization. Many people today evaluate Christ and Christianity according to their cultural and social impact in various parts of the world or in certain periods of history. This is what constitutes the historical aspect of Christianity, which can be appreciated and accepted by everyone.

There is another point of view that expresses the radicalism of many young people today, and it can be stated as follows: "Jesus Christ was a remarkable, exceptional and idealistic person, but what he stood for was a project that has never been fully realized, simply because the human being is essentially egotistic, arrogant, and violent." Consequently, many people today have come to the conclusion: "Jesus Christ, yes! The Church, no!" Still others have asserted that Jesus Christ was the first and only Christian!

The radical teaching of Christ—to give up everyone and everything, including oneself; the "folly" of the cross; the sacrifice of everything out of love and for love—seems too difficult to many, if not impossible. Unfortunately, many Christians think and live as if Jesus were only an unattainable ideal or as if his teaching was addressed to only a few, a privileged and select group such as clergy and persons in the consecrated life.

Let us take an example from the gospel. A rich young man faithfully followed Christ up to a certain point. He lived an exemplary life and could say to Jesus: "Teacher, I have kept all these since my childhood" (Mk 10:20). Blessed is he; he deserves the greatest respect and recognition!

"Then Jesus looked at him with love and told him: 'There is one thing more you must do. Go and sell what you have and give it to the poor; you will then have treasure in heaven. After that, come and follow me'" (Mk 10:21).

The rich young man had asked Jesus a very important, a decisive question: "Good teacher, what must I do to share in everlasting life?" (Mk 10:17). This is the same question that we should be asking at every moment of our life.

At the outset, the meeting of Jesus with the rich young man went very well, because the young man was faithful to the law of Moses; he was zealous and observant. That was very good for starters, but Jesus went farther. He probed the man's soul and offered him the opportunity to give up his earthly wealth in order to gain true wealth; to follow Jesus in poverty and to accept his own particular cross. Jesus wants to have him as a friend and brother, an intimate collaborator for the kingdom of heaven.

The offer made by Jesus is a compelling challenge: Jesus or riches! The young man chooses riches; he abandons Jesus, because he didn't have the courage to part with his riches. He was so attached to material goods that he could not understand nor accept the alternative choice offered to him, great as it was. "At these words the man's face fell. He went away sad, for he had many possessions" (Mk 10:22).

Let us examine this encounter and apply it to ourselves. Let us too ask Jesus what we must do, or better yet, how we should live in order to have eternal life, to attain salvation (cf. Mk 10:19). Let us listen to the response of Jesus, his directions that come to us from the gospel and the teaching of the Church, from life in our parish community and from our own voice of conscience.

Can we say with the rich young man that we have observed all these things from our childhood (cf. Mk 10:20)? In spite of our weaknesses and our sins of commission and omission, Jesus has chosen us to be his friends, his brothers and sisters (cf. Jn 15:14). But there is a condition: Jesus wants us to be free of everything and everyone. He wants us to follow him even to the cross and then to the resurrection, when we shall be definitively freed from sin, egoism, and every evil. So let us ask what we still need to do in order to know, love, follow and bear witness to Jesus.

Our vocation is Jesus. . . . God loves me; I am not in the world simply to occupy a certain place, only to be an added number. God has chosen me for a purpose. I know it; and I shall realize it if I do not place any obstacle in his way. But he will not force me. He could have forced the Virgin Mary, but he wanted Mary to say her yes. The same thing is true of us; God never forces us; he wants us to say yes. (Mother Teresa)

Today the Church and the world need authentic witnesses of Christ and the gospel, the testimony of a life that proves that the teaching of the gospel of Christ is possible and liveable, today and always. It can be done with the power of faith, the help of God, and by collaborating with our brothers and sisters.

What better response could there be to those who see Christianity and the Church only as related to culture, art, and the history of bygone days, preserved in library archives or museums! And the same holds true for those who are willing to accept Christ but not the Church.

If we live our faith intensely, we can bridge the distance between the historical Christ as recorded in the gospels and the Church as presented and preached today. For there is only one Christ, and there is only one Church, founded by Christ and made up of the faithful.

The Christian message is not only the message proclaimed by Christ and written in the gospels; it is the living word that arouses us and provokes a response and a choice.

Christ's invitation to holiness, humility, pardon, love of enemies, and perfection may seem difficult and even unattainable. Mother Teresa also had difficulties at the beginning of her "second vocation," the founding of the Missionaries of Charity. She had to endure patiently the initial refusal of the archbishop of Calcutta, the politico-social problems, the lack of understanding among the Sisters of Loreto, and the early negative attitude of the Holy See. This is the way she describes those "temptations against tranquillity":

I needed a roof for gathering the abandoned together. I got busy to look for one. . . . I walked and walked without break, until I could go no farther. Only then did I realize how exhausted the really poor must be, as they search for a bit of food, medicine or whatever. The memory of the physical comfort that I had enjoyed in the convent of Loreto came back to me now as a temptation. So I prayed: My God, by my free choice and by your love I want to remain here in order to do whatever your will asks of me. No, I shall not turn back. (Mother Teresa)

"God shows to men, in a vivid way, his presence and his face through the lives of those companions of ours . . . who are more perfectly transformed into the image of Christ. He speaks to us in them and offers us a sign of this, to which we are powerfully attracted, so great a cloud of witnesses is there given and such witness to the truth of the gospel" (LG 50).

This is not a privileged function given only to a few, such as the clergy; it is offered to all the baptized. Each and every lay person too should be a witness to the resurrection of Christ. The Second Vatican Council has stated that Christ has established the laity "as witnesses and provides them with the appreciation of the faith and the grace of the word so that the power of the gospel may shine out in daily family and social life" (LG 35). All together, and each one individually, should nourish the world with spiritual fruits and diffuse the spirit that animates the poor, the meek and the peacemakers, whom the Lord of the gospel has proclaimed as blessed. In a word, "what the soul is in the body, let Christians be in the world" (LG 38).

"The principal duty of both men and women is to bear witness to Christ, and this they are obliged to do by their life and their words, in the family, in their social group, and in the sphere of their profession. In them must be seen the new man who has been created according to God in justice and holiness of truth" (AG 21).

This is the mission of gospel witness. "Since Christians have different gifts, they should collaborate in the work of the gospel, each according to his opportunity, ability, charism and ministry" (AG 28).

"As members of the living Christ, incorporated into him and made like him by baptism, confirmation and the eucharist, all the faithful have an obligation to collaborate in the expansion and spread of his body, so that they might bring it to fullness as soon as possible. . . .

However, let everyone be aware that the primary and most important contribution he can make to the spread of the faith is to lead a profound Christian life. Their fervor in the service of God and their love for others . . . will appear as the sign raised above the nations, 'the light of the world' and 'the salt of the earth'" (AG 36).

You Will Be My Witnesses

Better for us to obey God rather than men!
The God of our fathers has raised up
Jesus whom you put to death, hanging
him on a tree. He whom God
has exalted at his right hand
as ruler and savior is to bring repentance
to Israel and forgiveness of sins.
We testify to this.
So too does the Holy Spirit, whom God
has given to those that obey him.
Acts of the Apostles 5:29-32

The essential thing is not what we say or
how we say it, but how we believe, live,
love and bear witness to Jesus.
Mother Teresa

To be witnesses, to give testimony, means to share with others who were not present what we have experienced. To give testimony is fundamental for our Christian faith; this is especially true of the primitive Christian witness, which goes all the way back to Christ, who died and rose again for our salvation.

Jesus had numerous followers and friends from whom he selected the twelve apostles and, later, his disciples. He was with them almost constantly during his public life, which lasted only three years. They had known him and had followed him closely as collaborators in the work of salvation (cf. DV 19).

The apostles and disciples had lived close to Jesus during the most important events of his public life (cf. LG 19). They witnessed his suffering, death and resurrection, and that is why our faith in these events is based on their testimony as recorded in scripture. Our faith rests likewise on the grace of the Holy Spirit and the teaching of the Church throughout the centuries.

To bear witness to Christ at the present time means not only to preach and to proclaim the death and resurrection of Christ. It entails something more: to make his presence felt. And how can we do that? In the same way the apostles and the early Christians did it, namely, by the testimony of our words and our life.

Our faith is based, as we have said, on the testimony of the apostles concerning that which they had seen and heard and followed closely. They were speaking from immediate experience. They gave testimony of these things to us not only in words but by their lives and even more by their deaths as martyrs. They sacrificed their own lives for the truth of the resurrection and the gospel. Hence, our faith is "apostolic"; it is based on and sustained by the Church of the apostles.

In addition to the testimony of the apostles, the testimony of sacred scripture is likewise very important for the Church. As a unique font of our salvation, it predicted the death and resurrection of Christ. This was confirmed by Jesus himself when he said to the disciples of Emmaus: "'How slow you are to believe all that the prophets have announced! Did not the Messiah have to undergo all this so as to enter into his glory?' Beginning, then, with Moses and all the prophets, he interpreted for them every passage of scripture which referred to him" (Lk 24:25-27). The death and resurrection of Christ is thus placed within the plan of salvation that was already announced and prefigured in the Old Testament.

In addition to the testimony of the apostles and that of sacred scripture, there is the testimony of the Holy Spirit, who supported and verified this truth and confirmed it with prodigious signs. Thus, when they were brought before the Sanhedrin, Peter and the apostles said: "We testify to this. So too does the Holy Spirit, whom God has given to those that obey him" (Acts 5:32). In other words, the Holy Spirit was present and active in the Church by his gifts. The powerful presence of the Holy Spirit and the preaching of the apostles were sufficient to arouse the faith in their hearers. Peter had proclaimed to them: "This is the Jesus God has raised up, and we are his witnesses. Exalted at God's right hand, he first received the promised Holy Spirit from the Father, then poured this Spirit out on us. This is what you now see and hear" (Acts 2:32-33).

Thus, the preaching of the apostles and the testimony from scripture were not sufficient for the faith of the early Church. Concrete facts and experience were also necessary, and these were supplied by the Holy Spirit. He gave courage and power to the apostles, and he aroused faith in those who listened to their preaching (cf. Acts 5:29-32). "With power the apostles bore witness to the resurrection of the Lord Jesus, and great respect was paid to them all" (Acts 4:33).

The apostolic preaching was accompanied by many prodigies and by numerous conversions. "Through the hands of the apostles, many signs and wonders occurred among the people. . . . The people held them in great esteem. . . . More and more believers, men and women in great numbers, were continually added to the Lord" (Acts 5:12-14).

The testimony of the apostles and the primitive Church that Christ has conquered death, sin and the devil is always with us, changing our lives and the destiny of humanity. Christ's resurrection is the cornerstone of the faith of the new community, which is gathered together by the power of the Holy Spirit. It too bears witness to this saving truth. Gathered around Christ by the power of the Holy Spirit, the early Church is born and then expands throughout the entire world. Paul states it this way: "Just as in Adam all die, so in Christ all will come to life again, but each one in proper order: Christ, the first fruits and then, at his coming, all those who belong to him" (1 Cor 15:22).

Jesus is in our midst not only through his teaching but especially through his life and his real presence in the Church and the sacraments. This makes possible a radical change of individuals, families and society as a whole. After the resurrection of Christ, believing means accepting the teaching that Jesus Christ is true God and true man; that he died and rose for us and for our salvation; that he is present among us, living and active, especially in the community of believers which is the Church. This means that we too can meet him, live him, love him and consequently attain salvation. Jesus has said: "I am the resurrection and the life; whoever believes in me, though he should die, will come to life; and whoever is alive and believes in me, will never die" (Jn 11:26).

The Church appreciates not only the importance of the early Christian witness but also the testimony of every single Christian's life. Thus salvation does not rest solely on historical facts but becomes the experience of every person in every age. This is the role of the Church in the history of humankind: to make Christ present in every time and place.

The original and irreplaceable function of faith is to give testimony, which is then communicated to others. Jesus also has come into the world to give witness to the truth, and he commanded the apostles to do the same. Their mission is therefore from the Father (cf. LG 35), through the Son (cf. Rv 1:5), in the Holy Spirit, to the apostles (cf. Jn 20:21), to the community of believers (cf. Jn 17:20), and ultimately to us through the Church.

The Second Vatican Council teaches: "The disciples of Christ, being in close contact with men through their life and work, hope to offer them an authentic Christian witness and work for their salvation. . . . So men are aided in attaining salvation by love of God and love of men" (AG 12).

"Works of charity and mercy bear a most striking testimony to Christian life; therefore, an apostolic training which has as its object the performance of these works should enable the faithful to learn from very childhood how to sympathize with their brothers, and help them generously when in need" (AA 31).

"Missionary activity is intimately bound up with human nature and its aspirations. In manifesting Christ, the Church reveals to men their true situation and calling, since Christ is the head and exemplar of that renewed humanity. . . . Christ is the truth and the way which the preaching of the gospel lays open to all men when it speaks those words of Christ in their ear: 'Repent, and believe the gospel' " (AG 8).

"Each individual layman must be a witness before the world to the resurrection and life of the Lord Jesus, and a sign of the living God" (LG 38).

All of our words will be useless if they do not come from the depths of the heart, if they are not confirmed by the witness of our life. . . . Therefore, the essential thing is not what we say or how we say it, but how we believe, live, love and bear witness to Jesus to others. . . . I always say to my Sisters: Carry Jesus wherever you go. I say the same to you and to all, and then others will be able to see Jesus in us. Then our life will be completely at the service of God, of the Church, and of humankind. (Mother Teresa)

With the Power of the Holy Spirit

*You will receive power
when the Holy Sprit comes down on you;
then you are to be my
witnesses in Jerusalem,
throughout Judea and Samaria,
yes, even to the ends of the earth.*
Acts of the Apostles 1:8

*If we want to conquer the world,
we cannot do it with bombs
or any other weapons of destruction.
Let us conquer the world with our love.
Let us weave into our lives the links
of the chain of sacrifice and of love;
then it will be possible
for us to conquer the world.*
Mother Teresa

The risen Christ was for the apostles and the primitive Christian community an inexhaustible source of joy, strength and life. He was the principal cause of their union with God and neighbor and among themselves. To celebrate his resurrection, the community frequently gathered together in common prayer and celebrated the eucharist. Sunday was the beginning of the week, and on that day they celebrated the mystery of their redemption, their liberation from evil and sin. Thus the community grew in faith and love, and in union with God and each other.

This same methodology is still valid and necessary for the Christian community today. Without the presence of the risen Christ, without prayer and the eucharist, there is no Christian community, no Church.

Jesus explicitly commanded the apostles to bear witness of him to the world, and in order that they could do so, he promised to send the Holy Spirit to them. The apostles did not yet fully understand all that Jesus had said and done. It was only after the resurrection that they thought the opportune time had arrived to restore the kingdom of Israel. After so much uncertainty, fear and suffering, the sun of consolation, namely Christ, had finally risen and was present in their midst.

"While they were with him they asked,

'Lord, are you going to restore the rule to Israel now?' His answer was: 'The exact time is not yours to know. The Father has reserved that to himself'" (Acts 1:6-7).

The Acts of the Apostles is an authentic witness of the life, faith and love of the primitive Church. It describes the community of the baptized in Jerusalem, the preaching of Peter, and the work of Paul among the Gentiles. Some Bible scholars call the Acts of the Apostles "the gospel according to the Holy Spirit," because it describes his role in the Church, which carries on the work of salvation.

The Holy Spirit is the leading actor in this marvelous and beautiful history, which is a testimony of the fruitful collaboration of humanity with God. After having demonstrated in so many ways that he was truly risen, Jesus told the apostles not to leave Jerusalem. "Wait, rather, for the fulfillment of my Father's promise, of which you have heard me speak" (Acts 1:4).

Some time before this, Jesus had said to them: "I did indeed come from the Father; I came into the world. Now I am leaving the world to go to the Father" (Jn 16:28). In accordance with Christ's command, the immediate task of the apostles was to prepare for the coming of the Holy Spirit, the new baptism; then to bear witness to the life and work of Christ. And the fruit of the Holy Spirit was an ardent love for God and neighbor, as we read in the description of the primitive Christian community:

"They devoted themselves to the apostles' instruction and the communal life, to the breaking of bread and the prayers. . . . Those who believed shared all things in common; they would sell their property and goods, dividing everything on the basis of each one's need. They went to the temple area together every day, while in their homes they broke bread. With exultant and sincere hearts they took their meals in common, praising God and winning the approval of all the people. Day by day the Lord added to their number those who were being saved" (Acts 2:42-47).

From the foregoing description we can summarize some important practical points:

1) The dedication of the apostles to preaching means that they had a special concern for the word of God, for bearing witness to the life and deeds of Christ. We too should have a special concern for the Bible, the word of God, without which there can be no education and growth in the faith (cf. DV 21).

Spiritual reading, especially of the Bible, is one of the spiritual exercises and duties that is most precious to us, so much so that no one may ever neglect it. Jesus speaks to us today through the gospel, in meditation, adoration and prayer. It is not merely a written word, a dead word; it is the word of life. The word becomes flesh during the day at meditation, in holy communion, in contemplation, adoration and silence. If we nourish ourselves daily with sacred scripture, and especially the New Testament, we shall grow in the knowledge and love of Jesus. . . . The word of God, which is in us, we shall give to others. (Mother Teresa)

2) They devoted themselves to community gatherings, the breaking of bread and to prayer. There were various kinds of community gatherings: with the apostles, with the disciples of

Jesus, with immediate witnesses. The eucharist, however, was of capital importance. They spoke of it as "the breaking of bread" and prayer. Here we have the pillars of the community life: Jesus in the eucharist and the practice of prayer (cf. LG 3).

"Because the loaf of bread is one, we, many though we are, are one body, for we all partake of the one loaf" (1 Cor 10:17). Today we also come together for community gatherings, for daily and weekly meetings, and especially on Sundays for the celebration of the eucharist, the mystery of our faith. There we proclaim the death and resurrection of Christ; we are nourished by his presence and love; we pray together.

My great love is Jesus in the eucharist, in holy communion. There I meet him, I receive him, I love him; then I re-discover him and serve him in the poorest of the poor. Without daily communion my life would be empty, useless; my work would be superfluous. . . . Only with assiduous prayer and with communion are we able to live with Jesus and for Jesus with our poor and for our poor and needy. (Mother Teresa)

3) They held everything in common, because there was neither rich nor poor among them; everyone was equal, like brothers and sisters. Today this message seems to be only a beautiful memory, an idealistic story. The world of today is different in so many ways. There are few rich but so many poor; few privileged but so many marginalized; many slaves and few free. If Christ is always timely and relevant, if the gospel is the word of life for all, then it ought to apply to all today, in our time and place.

In order to correct and remedy some of these injustices, from the time of the apostles the Church has always had a special care for the poor, the sick, the rejected, the oppressed, and for all who are threatened in any way. Today the Church still follows this direction by means of various apostolates and religious organizations. The world today needs our Christian witness at the level of public and social service, where love and solidarity must find new ways of being realized.

"In the early days the Church linked the 'agape' to the eucharistic supper, and by so doing showed itself as one body around Christ united by the bond of charity. So too, in all ages, love is its characteristic mark. While rejoicing at initiatives taken elsewhere, it claims charitable works as its own mission and right. That is why mercy to the poor and the sick, and charitable works and works of mutual aid for the alleviation of all kinds of human needs, are held in special honor in the Church" (AA 8).

4) The community grew day by day with new members. This growth was not only numerical but also in depth, in faith and love. In like manner, by the power of the Holy Spirit, the Church continues to grow today (cf. Acts 1:8).

Pentecost: the Birth of the Church

When the day of Pentecost came it found them gathered in one place. Suddenly from up in the sky there came a noise like a strong, driving wind which was heard all through the house where they were seated. Tongues of fire appeared, which parted and came to rest on each of them. All were filled with the Holy Spirit. They began to express themselves in foreign tongues and make bold proclamation as the Spirit prompted them.

Acts of the Apostles 2:1-4

As we prepare ourselves for the coming of the Holy Spirit, I pray for you that the Holy Spirit will be able to fill you with his power, grace and purity so that you will be able to see the face of God in one another and in the faces of the poor that you serve.

Mother Teresa

With Peter at the head and together with the Virgin Mary, the apostles were gathered together in Jerusalem, awaiting in prayer the coming of the Holy Spirit in accordance with the promise of Jesus. They are now certain about the resurrection of Jesus, for they have had various direct contacts with him (cf. Mt 28:1-10; Mk 16:1-8; Lk 24:1-49; Jn 20:1-10).

Jesus had told them not to leave Jerusalem until the descent of the Holy Spirit. The apostles did not simply wait passively for this to happen. As the gospel says, they prepared themselves: "Together they devoted themselves to constant prayer. There were some women in their company, and Mary the mother of Jesus, and his brothers" (Acts 1:14). At the same time a large crowd had come to Jerusalem from all parts of the Hebrew diaspora of the world. They had come as pilgrims to the holy city in order to gather together in the temple and give witness to their common faith. The pilgrimage was part of the celebration of the feast of Thanksgiving for benefits received from God, and in particular for the fruits of the earth (cf. Ex 23:16; 34:21). It was also an occasion to recall the covenant established on Mount Sinai and the history of the Chosen People.

The miracle of the descent of the Holy Spirit was announced by external signs. The "noise like a strong driving wind" was an indication of new life and new power conferred on the apostles. The "tongues of fire" signified that now it was time for a new language, and the fire had to purify the old and destroy the power of evil and of sin. The various "foreign tongues" were the verification of a new community, a new people of God, the Church, which embraces all languages, cultures and races. The unity of the Church is not the fruit of human endeavor, however, but of divine power. The Holy Spirit is the source of unity of faith and love amid diversity.

The events at Pentecost also aroused great interest among the people in Jerusalem: "Staying in Jerusalem at the time were devout Jews of every nation under the heaven. These heard the sound and assembled in a large crowd. They were much confused because each one heard these men speaking his own language. The whole occurrence astonished them. . . . They were dumbfounded and could make nothing at all of what had happened. 'What does this mean?' they asked one another, while a few remarked with a sneer, 'They have had too much new wine!' " (Acts 2:5-6; 12-13).

Then Peter stood up, and in the name of God and of the apostles he told the people what had happened. "You who are Jews, indeed all of you staying in Jerusalem! Listen to what I have to say. You must realize that these men are not drunk, as you seem to think. It is only nine in the morning! No, it is what Joel the prophet spoke of" (Acts 2:14-16).

Peter then went on to explain: "Jesus the Nazarean was a man whom God sent to you with miracles, wonders, and signs as his credentials. These God worked through him in your midst, as you well know. He was delivered up by the set purpose and plan of God; you even

made use of pagans to crucify and kill him. God freed him from death's bitter pangs, however, and raised him up again, for it was impossible that death should keep its hold on him. . . . Therefore let the whole house of Israel know beyond any doubt that God has made both Lord and Messiah this Jesus whom you crucified" (Acts 2:22-24; 36).

This courageous and clear public testimony aroused even greater amazement among the people, as well as regret for the crucifixion of Jesus. At the same time it was for many a cause for joy and faith in his resurrection. So the people then asked Peter what they should do to make amends, and Peter responded: "You must reform and be baptized, each one of you, in the name of Jesus Christ, that your sins may be forgiven; then you will receive the gift of the Holy Spirit. It was to you and your children that the promise was made, and to all those still far off whom the Lord our God calls" (Acts 2:38-39).

In his reply Peter places great emphasis on the need for conversion, repentance and penance in order to make reparation for sin and also "that your sins may be forgiven" (Acts 2:38).

Conversion does not mean only the admission of our sins; more than that, it requires that we acknowledge the infinite goodness and mercy of God, who pardons us. For the conversion of the people of Israel it was necessary to acknowledge Jesus Christ as Messiah and Savior. This was an essential condition for the reception of baptism or, as Peter had said, to "receive the gift of the Holy Spirit" (Acts 2:38). And here once again it is evident that the Holy Spirit was not sent to the apostles only, but to all who believe in Jesus Christ. In fact, Jesus himself had said: "I did not come to condemn the world but to save it" (Jn 12:47).

Paul says: "I am not ashamed of the gospel. It is the power of God leading everyone who believes in it to salvation, the Jew first, then the Greek. For in the gospel is revealed the justice of God, which begins and ends with faith; as scripture says, 'The just man shall live by faith'" (Rm 1:16-17).

In the primitive Church two principal events called for faith: the resurrection of Christ and the descent of the Holy Spirit. In other words, belief in the resurrection of Christ, which is the paschal mystery, and belief in the gift of the Holy Spirit, which makes possible the salvation of all the people in the world, through the Church as "the sacrament of unity and of salvation" (cf. LG 1, 9, 48).

Mother Teresa said:

Ask the Holy Spirit to make you sinners without sin. . . . We should bear witness to the change, to conversion, with joy. Joy is a fruit of the Holy Spirit, a sign that he dwells within us. Jesus bestowed joy on his disciples: "All this I tell you that my joy may be yours and your joy may be complete" (Jn 15:11). Our joy is the fruit of generosity, the absence of egoism, of close union with God. God bestows on us the greatest gift—the Holy Spirit—after having given us Jesus. And we are called to give ourselves freely to God and to neighbor with generosity and joy.

The Second Vatican Council teaches: "Just as Christ was sent by the Father so also he sent the apostles, filled with the Holy Spirit. He did this so that they might preach the gospel to every creature and proclaim that by his death and resurrection the Son of God has freed us from the power of Satan and from death. . . .

He also willed that the work of salvation which they preached should be set in train through the sacrifice and sacraments, around which the entire liturgical life revolves" (SC 6).

"They were fully confirmed in this mission on the day of Pentecost, according to the promise of the Lord: 'You shall receive power when the Holy Spirit descends upon you; and you shall be my witnesses both in Jerusalem and in all Judea and Samaria, and to the remotest part of the earth' (Acts 1:8). By preaching everywhere the gospel, welcomed and received under the influence of the Holy Spirit by those who hear it, the apostles gather together the universal Church, which the Lord founded upon the apostles and built upon blessed Peter their leader, the chief cornerstone being Christ Jesus himself" (LG 19).

The Second Vatican Council further comments on the mission of the apostles: "On the day of Pentecost, however, he came down upon the disciples that he might remain with them forever; on that day the Church was openly displayed to the crowds, and the spread of the gospel among the nations, through preaching, was begun. Finally, on that day was foreshadowed the union of all peoples in the catholicity of the faith by means of the Church of the New Alliance, a Church which speaks every language, understands and embraces all tongues in charity, and thus overcomes the dispersion of Babel" (AG 4).

In essence the Church is Jesus, while we are only the external part. It is we, men and women who are part of the Church, who need money and property; but Jesus doesn't need anything. May God grant, through the work of the Holy Spirit, that we may be open to the ways that lead us beyond ourselves. (Mother Teresa)

The Church in the World

*Go, therefore, and make disciples
of all the nations. Baptize them
in the name "of the Father, and of the Son,
and of the Holy Spirit."
Teach them to carry out everything
I have commanded you.
And know that I am with you always,
until the end of the world.*
Mark 28:19-20

*This is our mission:
to make God present in the world of today
by our life and witness.*
Mother Teresa

Great works are not limited by space and time. They have an immortal and universal value, and for that reason they are handed down from one generation to another, from one people to another, from one age to all ages. Those who have created or performed such great works become famous throughout the world because they have left their mark on the history of humanity. Think, for example, of those who are immortal in the field of music, such as Vivaldi, Bach, Beethoven, Mozart and others. Their music has surpassed the confines of time and peoples; it is now a treasure that belongs to humanity at large. And there are numerous other gifted individuals who have immortalized themselves in prose and poetry, painting and sculpture, architecture and other branches of the fine arts.

Similarly, Christ's work of salvation, particularly his death and resurrection, is not restricted in time and space only to the contemporaries of Jesus or to the Jews alone. His saving work is carried on through the Church. At Pentecost the nucleus of the Church was formed, and even then it comprised a variety of peoples, languages, cultures and traditions. Since then the Good News has been proclaimed far beyond the confines of Israel.

By the power of the Holy Spirit the primitive Christian community at Jerusalem announced the resurrection of Christ and testified to salvation. As a result, Peter and John were arrested and imprisoned (cf. Acts 4:1-22; 5:17-42). But to give witness necessarily calls for sacrifice and suffering, as Jesus had to endure in giving witness to the Father. The deacon Stephen was also condemned and ultimately killed because he preached and testified to the resurrection of Christ (cf. Acts 7:54-60).

Persecution spread rapidly to other Christian communities, and Saul of Tarsus was known to many of the churches as a zealous persecutor of Christians. It was on one of his journeys for this purpose that he had a vision and an encounter with the risen Christ. "As he traveled along and was approaching Damascus, a light from the sky suddenly flashed about him. He fell to the ground and at the same time heard a voice saying, 'Saul, Saul, why do you persecute me?' 'Who are you, sir?' he asked. The voice answered, 'I am Jesus, the one you are persecuting. Get up and go into the city, where you will be told what to do'" (Acts 9:3-6).

Saul on that occasion lost the sight of his bodily eyes, but it was in order for him to see spiritually by faith. He went to Damascus as commanded, and there Ananias restored his eyesight. "He got up and was baptized, and his strength returned to him after he had taken food" (Acts 9:18).

When the other Christians heard what had happened to Saul, they were astonished. "Any who heard it were greatly taken aback. They kept saying: 'Isn't this the man who worked such havoc in Jerusalem among those who invoke this name? Did he not come here purposely to apprehend such people and bring them before the chief priests?'" (Acts 9:21).

Behold how Jesus selected Saul and changed him from an enemy to a friend, as is stated in the Acts of the Apostles: "This man is the instrument I have chosen to bring my name to the Gentiles and their kings and to the people of Israel" (Acts 9:15).

The persecuted Christians spread to Antioch in Syria and began to proclaim the gospel there. It was in Antioch that the first Christian community outside Jerusalem was established. "Some men of Cyprus and Cyrene among them who had come to Antioch began to talk even to the Greeks, announcing the good news of the Lord Jesus to them. The hand of the Lord was with them and a great number of them believed and were converted to the Lord. . . . It was in Antioch that the disciples were called Christians for the first time" (Acts 11:20-21, 26).

From the very beginning, the Church was faced with two realities: The Jewish world, which was scattered throughout various parts of the Mediterranean and other parts of the earth; and the pagan or Gentile world, as it is called in scripture. The people of Israel are now no longer the exclusive people of God; in fact, they now have a missionary vocation in regard to all other peoples. And this new union with all of humanity is realized in Jesus Christ, thus creating a new people of God, a new Israel, the Church.

This opening toward all peoples is necessary for the Church at all times, and hence for our times also. We are all called to salvation or, as the Second Vatican Council puts it: "Christ is the light of humanity" (LG 1). But some of the baptized Jews reacted very strongly against the baptized Gentiles. According to them, the pagans should first have embraced Judaism and then passed on to the Christian religion, as they themselves had done (cf. Acts 10:44-46). This gave rise to a serious problem: How should the Church respond to pagan Gentiles who want to be baptized? The question called for an immediate, precise response that was in accordance with the will of Christ.

"The apostles and the presbyters accordingly convened to look into the matter. After much discussion, Peter took the floor and said to them: 'Brothers, you know well enough that from the early days God selected me from your number to be the one from whose lips the Gentiles would hear the message of the gospel and believe. God, who reads the hearts of men, showed his approval by granting the Holy Spirit to them just as he did to us. He made no distinction between them and us, but purified their hearts by means of faith also. Why, then, do you put God to the test by trying to place on the shoulders of these converts a yoke which neither we nor our fathers were able to bear? Our belief is rather that we are saved by the favor of the Lord Jesus and so are they'" (Acts 15:6-11).

This statement was supported also by Paul and Barnabas, and by James as well (cf. Acts 15:12, 15-19). Then the entire assembly and the Church at Jerusalem agreed on a decision, and they decreed that Judas (known as Barsabbas) and Silas should accompany Paul and Barnabas to Antioch and deliver the letter containing the decision:

"The apostles and the presbyters, your brothers, send greetings to the brothers of Gentile origin in Antioch, Syria, and Cilicia. We have heard that some of our number without any instruction from us have upset you with their discussions and disturbed your peace of mind. Therefore we have unanimously resolved to choose representatives and send them to you, along with our beloved Barnabas and Paul, who have dedicated themselves to the cause of our Lord Jesus Christ. Those whom we are sending you are Judas and Silas, who will convey this message by word of mouth: 'It is the decision of the Holy Spirit, and ours too, not to lay on you any burden beyond that which is strictly necessary, namely, to abstain from meat sacrificed to idols, from blood, from the meat of strangled animals, and from illicit sexual union. You will be well advised to avoid these things. Farewell'" (Acts 15:23-29).

This decision by the Council of Jerusalem was very important, because it opened the Church to the world while remaining faithful to Jesus Christ under the inspiration of the Holy Spirit. It also highlighted the decisive role of the Holy Spirit in the Church, the primacy of Peter as head of the apostles, and the significance of the experience and testimony of Paul and Barnabas.

To preach the gospel or to evangelize does not mean simply to talk about the gospel, but to give the Good News, the news of salvation, to others, and to bear witness to that by one's own life and experience. "This is what we proclaim to you: What was from the beginning, what we have heard, what we have seen with our eyes, what we have looked upon and our hands have touched—we speak of the word of life. (This life became visible; we have seen and bear witness to it, and we proclaim to you the eternal life that was present to the Father and became visible to us.) What we have seen and heard we proclaim in turn to you so that you may share life with us" (1 Jn 1:1-3).

Authentic witness must spring from the experience of faith and from the universality and catholicity of the Church, because "as all the members of the human body, though they are many, form one body, so also are the faithful in Christ (cf. 1 Cor 12:12)" (LG 7).

"It is the Holy Spirit, dwelling in those who believe and pervading and ruling over the entire Church, who brings about that wonderful communion of the faithful and joins them together so intimately in Christ that he is the principle of the Church's unity" (UR 2).

And Jesus says: As the Father has loved me and gives me to the world, so I have loved you and give my life for you. Remain in my love, giving of yourselves (cf. Jn 15:9). This giving of oneself is prayer; the sacrifice of charity is poverty; obedience, free service offered with all one's heart. We should love to the extent that we are disposed to suffer. It is not enough to say "I love." We should translate that love into dynamic activity. And how can we do that? By giving of ourselves to the point of suffering. (Mother Teresa)

The Church: One and Holy

It was in one Spirit that all of us, whether Jew or Greek, slave or free, were baptized into one body. All of us have been given to drink of the one Spirit.
1 Corinthians 12:13

The unity of the Church and in the Church is not an artificial uniformity but a unity of life to be lived. Consequently there is only one thing that interests me: We should all be collaborators of Jesus Christ, because if we are united with him, we shall easily and naturally be united among ourselves.
Mother Teresa

Founded by Christ and confirmed by the Holy Spirit, the Church faithfully carries on the work of salvation in human history. As such, it is the means, the instrument, and the sacrament of salvation.

In the Creed we profess this truth: "We believe in one holy, catholic and apostolic Church" (CCC, p. 50). The Creed also refers to the work of salvation when it states that Jesus rose from the dead. Consequently, the nucleus of the Creed is christological; we confess and accept Christ as Savior and Redeemer. Ambrose said: "The Church is the expression of the Father, through the Son and in the Holy Spirit."

As the sacrament of salvation, the Church continues the work of Jesus as "a sign and instrument of communion with God and of unity among all men" (LG 1; GS 42). Christ is the greatest and most intimate bond of union with God and with humanity, since he himself is true God and true man. The Church is the sign and the means of this twofold unity; it is the universal sacrament of salvation (cf. LG 48; AG 5).

Paul VI expressed this truth in this way: "The Church is the visible sign of God's love for humanity, the sacrament of salvation." The same truth was foretold in the Old Testament through the people of Israel, who passed from a nomadic life to the diaspora among other peoples, then to messianism and finally to a missionary proclamation to the whole world. The Church is perfectly prefigured and prepared for in the biblical context. In a certain way it appears in the life and history of the Chosen People even before its foundation and historical existence.

In the New Testament the Church appears as a new way to experience God and relate to one's neighbor, realized in Jesus Christ and in the community of the apostles. In fact, the Church breaks out of and transcends its Judaic mold by reason of many new divine elements. This awareness of a "new people of God" is expressed by various new concepts; for example, "the body of Christ," "God with us," "a new humanity" comprised of Jews and Gentiles, of all who believe in Jesus Christ.

Augustine describes the Church as "the means of reconciliation with God and with neighbor." Paul writes: "Just as each of us has one body with many members, and not all the members have the same function, so too we, though many, are one body in Christ and individually members one of another" (Rm 12:4-5). "It is he [Christ] who is head of the body, the Church; he who is the beginning, the firstborn of the dead, so that primacy may be his in everything" (Col 1:18; cf. LG 3).

The Church is one

As God is one in the Most Holy Trinity, so also Christ willed and founded the one Church under the headship of the apostle Peter, after Peter's triple denial and his triple expression of repentance and love (cf. Jn 21:15-17; Mt 28:18).

Similarly, the unity of the Church has three modalities:

1) Unity of teaching and witness of the faith. We all believe in the same way the truths revealed by Jesus Christ, transmitted by the apostles, and taught and defined by the magisterium of the Church and by tradition. We are all called to live in accordance with the truth of the gospel and thus witness to Christ everywhere today.

"Christ the Lord founded one Church and one Church only" (UR 1). This unity is fostered and manifested in the Church's sacramental and liturgical life. "Liturgical services are not private functions but are celebrations of the Church, which is 'the sacrament of unity,' namely, 'the holy people united and arranged under their bishops'" (SC 26).

The eucharist especially is "the wonderful sacrament by which the unity of the Church is both signified and brought about. He gave his followers a new commandment to love one another, and promised the Spirit, their Advocate, who, as Lord and life-giver, should remain with them forever" (UR 2).

The Second Vatican Council has declared: "This is the sole Church of Christ, which in the Creed we profess to be one, holy, catholic and apostolic, which our Savior, after his resurrection, entrusted to Peter's pastoral care, commissioning him and the other apostles to extend and rule it, and which he raised up for all ages as 'the pillar and mainstay of the truth'" (LG 8).

2) Unity of the communal celebration of the liturgy, of the Mass and the sacraments.

3) Unity of mutual love as the family of God (cf. UR 2).

The Church is holy

The holiness of the Church is derived from its founder, Jesus Christ, who died and rose again to free us from evil. And Christ himself has told us: "You must be made perfect as your heavenly Father is perfect" (Mt 5:48).

"The Church, to which we are all called in Christ Jesus, and in which by the grace of God we acquire holiness, will receive its perfection only in the glory of heaven, when will come the time of renewal of all things. At that time, together with the human race, the universe itself, which is so closely related to man and which attains its destiny through him, will be perfectly reestablished in Christ" (LG 48; cf. UR 4).

Paul writes: "It is God's will that you grow in holiness: that you abstain from immorality" (1 Thes 4:3). He then goes on to say: "Over all these virtues put on love, which binds the rest together and makes them perfect" (Col 3:14).

Perfection, or holiness, has been a mark of the Church all through the centuries, down to the present day. God manifests himself, acts and is present in our midst through the saints. In this way he indicates to us the road we should follow. Thus, our holy brothers and sisters are models, helps, and inspiration for us.

A very special kind of holiness is found in the Virgin Mary, the Queen of angels and saints. Mother Teresa spoke of Mary when she visited her native city of Skopje in Albania in 1978:

All of us have one Father, the heavenly Father, and one Mother, Our Lady. Religious are at the very heart of our holy Mother Church; they are servants of the Lord, as the Virgin Mary was. . . . The unique source of unity and holiness is Jesus in the eucharist. . . . By nourishing ourselves on his body and blood, we shall become one body with Jesus and through Jesus, thanks to his great love. . . . Holiness is not the privilege of a few; it is a duty for every Christian, for me and for you. Our work is a marvelous means for our sanctification. . . . With holiness you will be able to love and serve others in your and my city of Skopje. (Mother Teresa)

She then went on to say:

This is the holiness of everyday life: to live in peace and in love with God and our neighbor, to help all those who have need of our hands, our words, our smile, our heart; to be always ready for sacrifice, for service, for love. That is a very simple but a profound and authentic holiness. Only holiness can make us capable of perfect sacrifice, of total giving. What is a saint? A resolute soul; a soul that makes use of its power for action. Paul did not intend to say anything else when he affirmed: "I can do all things in him who strengthens me." (Mother Teresa)

The Church: Catholic and Apostolic

Catholicity or universality is a characteristic of the Church founded by Christ. It seems that Ignatius of Antioch was the first to call the Church "catholic." He wrote: "Where Christ is, there is the catholic Church."

But what does it mean to be catholic, or to be part of the Catholic Church today? The catholicity of the Church is a rich term that can be expressed in a variety of ways:

— The universal character of the Church distinguishes and describes the new people of God, formed out of many peoples on earth by the Holy Spirit.

"The one people of God is accordingly present in all the nations of the earth, since its citizens, who are taken from all nations, are of a kingdom whose nature is not earthly but heavenly. All the faithful scattered throughout the world are in communion with each other in the Holy Spirit so that 'he who dwells in Rome knows those in most distant parts to be his members. . . .' This character of universality which adorns the people of God is a gift from the Lord himself whereby the Catholic Church ceaselessly and efficaciously seeks for the return of all humanity and all its goods under Christ the head in the unity of his Spirit" (LG 13).

— Through the Church Christ is present in the world, for he is "head of the Church, which is his body; the fullness of him who fills the universe in all its parts" (Eph 1:22).

— The mission of the Church is the same as that of Christ: the salvation of the world (cf. Mt 28:19); consequently, we are all called to take part in the history of salvation (LG 13).

Catholicity does not lessen or destroy unity; it actually increases the unity of charity. "In all things let charity prevail. If they are true to this course of action, they will be giving ever richer expression to the authentic catholicity and apostolicity of the Church" (UR 4). Then, amid the diversity of peoples, languages, cultures, traditions, and races, catholicity and unity enrich the Church's experience on the road to salvation (cf. LG 23).

The catholicity of the Church is closely connected to the Church's apostolicity. The Church is called and truly is "apostolic," because it is founded on the apostles under the primacy of Peter. Thus, Paul writes: "You form a building which rises on the foundation of the apostles and prophets, with Christ Jesus himself as the capstone. Through him the whole structure is fitted together and takes shape as a holy temple in the Lord; in him you are being built into this temple, to become a dwelling place for God in the Spirit" (Eph 2:20-22).

"This mystery [the death and resurrection of Christ] was not made known to other generations as it has now been revealed to his holy apostles and prophets by the Holy Spirit" (DV 17).

Jesus definitely chose the apostles, and from their midst he selected Peter as the head of the apostles and of the Church. This can be verified from many references in the New Testament:

— There is mention of the first among the apostles (cf. Mt 10:12), who gave testimony to the divinity and messianic mission of Christ in these words: "You are the Messiah, the Son of the living God" (Mt 16:16; Mk 8:27; Lk 9:18; Jn 6:67).

— Jesus publicly said to Peter: "I for my part declare to you, you are 'Rock,' and on this rock I will build my Church, and the jaws of death shall not prevail against it. I will entrust to you the keys of the kingdom of heaven. Whatever you declare bound on earth shall be bound in heaven; whatever you declare loosed on earth shall be loosed in heaven" (Mt 16:18-19).

— Peter was also the first to acknowledge Jesus as Messiah at the miraculous drought of fish (Lk 5:3) and then to hear the words addressed to him by Christ: "I have prayed for you that your faith may never fail. You in turn must strengthen your brothers" (Lk 22:32).

— Jesus entrusted his flock to Peter (cf. Jn 21:15-18). And Paul gives this testimony: "I handed on to you first of all what I myself received, that Christ died for our sins in accordance with the scriptures; that he was buried and, in accordance with the scriptures, rose on the third day; that he was seen by Cephas, then by the Twelve" (1 Cor 15:3-5).

The mission of Peter can be noted everywhere: in the time of the apostles, in the early Church, in the faith and tradition of the Church, in the teaching of the magisterium. This same mission and guidance has been handed on to the successors of Peter in the person of the Pope, Bishop of Rome. Thus, the Second Vatican Council has stated: "The Lord Jesus, having prayed at length to the Father, called to himself those whom he willed and appointed twelve to be with him, whom he might send to preach the kingdom of God. . . . These apostles he constituted in the form of a college or permanent assembly, at the head of which he placed Peter, chosen from amongst them" (LG 19; 20-21).

The role of the bishops and the pope was again confirmed by the Second Vatican Council: "Just as, in accordance with the Lord's decree, Peter and the rest of the apostles constitute a unique apostolic college, so in like fashion the Roman Pontiff, Peter's successor, and the bishops, the successors of the apostles, are related with and united to one another. . . . The college or body of bishops has for all that no authority unless united with the Roman Pontiff, Peter's successor, as its head, whose primatial authority, let it be added, over all, whether pastors or faithful, remains in its integrity" (LG 22).

The relationship of individual bishops with the pope is expressed this way: "The individual bishops are the visible source and foundation of unity in their own particular churches, which are constituted after the model of the universal Church; it is in these and formed out of them that the one and unique Catholic Church exists. And for that reason precisely each bishop represents his own church whereas all, together with the pope, represent the whole Church in a bond of peace, love and unity" (LG 23).

The Blessed Virgin Mary has a special role in the Church. Pope Paul VI said: "We believe that the blessed Mother of God, the new Eve, the Mother of the Church, continues her maternal care for all the members of the Church."

The Church follows us and supports us at every moment of our life, until we go to the Father. And we, you and I, do we have a care and love for our Mother? Are we worthy sons and daughters of this loving Mother? (Mother Teresa)

Mother Teresa loves the Church, the pope, the bishops and priests, everyone. She received permission from Pope Pius XII to found a new religious institute, Missionaries of Charity, in 1950. Then, with the *Decretum laudis* in 1965, the Congregation was recognized as a pontifical institute. When Pope Paul VI visited India, he gave the Sisters his automobile, which proved to be a great help in caring for the lepers. In 1968 Pope Paul VI personally invited Mother Teresa to open a house in Rome, and he paid for her round-trip ticket between Calcutta and Rome. In 1971 he bestowed on her the medal of Pope John XXIII for peace.

Speaking about the house in Rome, Mother once said to me:

I was not very much convinced that there would be poor people in Rome, but when the pope asked me, I could not refuse. During our conversation I said to him: "Your Holiness, I am ready to open a house if there are poor people." After visiting the Eternal City, I went back to the Pope and said to him: "Your Holiness, God has put aside work for us everywhere."

Mother Teresa had a very filial relationship with Pope John Paul II. Here are a few examples. After receiving the Nobel Peace Prize, she told me that she would retire from public life and return to the care of the lepers. The Pope did not permit her to do that; instead, he asked her to witness to the gospel all over the world. In his words, he wanted her to be "a living gospel and an authentic witness of a life consecrated to God and to the suffering neighbor."

In 1980 Pope John Paul II invited Mother Teresa to take part in the Synod of Bishops,

where she delivered an important and moving discourse in the presence of the Holy Father and bishops from all over the world. Among other things, she said: "The world today and all of us need holy priests."

The Holy Father's pastoral visit to India in 1986 was especially important for the Church, because he visited so many poor and wretched parts of the country. He wanted to meet Mother Teresa in her own surroundings at Calcutta, so he visited the house of the dying and gave words of encouragement to Mother Teresa and the Missionaries of Charity. In 1989 the Holy Father gave Mother Teresa a house for the poor and abandoned of Rome, situated near the Audience Hall of Paul VI, under the title "Gift of Mary."

On April 25, 1993, when he stopped at Shkodra in Albania during a pastoral visit, the Holy Father spoke from the balcony of the archbishop's residence after celebrating Mass. He publicly greeted and thanked Mother Teresa in the name of the Church for her life and work of Christian charity. On that occasion he said: "I cannot neglect to greet a very humble person who is here among us. She is Mother Teresa of Calcutta. Everyone knows where she comes from, what is her native land. The whole world knows that Mother Teresa is Albanian, your daughter, the incarnation of Christian love for the suffering and poor of the world."

Later, Mother Teresa wrote to the Sisters:

The Holy Father received me with great affection and later we prayed together. He has asked of us loyalty to Christ and to the Church. He asked for our prayers for his mission in the world. I told him about our poor, our sick and our lepers. He travels very much and works much for the Church and for peace. Wherever the Pope has gone, he has increased faith, hope and love. We should pray for the Holy Father, love him and help him in his difficult mission for the Church and for the world by our prayers, our sacrifices, our life and our obedience to the Vicar of Christ.

The Missionary Church

*The missionary ought to die each day
if she wants to bring souls to God.
She should be ready to pay the price
that he paid for souls and follow
the pathways that he trod.
Our holy faith is nothing else
but a gospel of love:
to manifest the love of God for humanity
and to ask for the love of all in exchange.*
Mother Teresa

By her very nature the Church was and always will be a missionary Church, in accordance with the command of Christ. As he was sent by the Father, he sent his apostles to proclaim to all the gospel of salvation, peace and love. To be a missionary means first of all to be chosen, to be sent on a mission, to announce a message. The whole Church has been sent by Christ to bring Christ to the world, to preach the message of salvation.

The first real missionary was Jesus Christ, who was obedient to the Father through the work of the Holy Spirit. The early Church soon spread from Jerusalem to Antioch, to Rome, to Greece and to other regions of the Middle East. Paul was an outstanding missionary, and on one occasion he was the recipient of a vision and a dramatic appeal: "One night Paul had a vision. A man of Macedonia stood before him and invited him, 'Come over to Macedonia and help us.' After this vision, we immediately made efforts to get across to Macedonia, concluding that God had summoned us to proclaim the good news there" (Acts 16:9-10).

Arriving at Neapolis and later at Philippi, a leading city of Macedonia, they spoke to a group of women who were gathered at a place of prayer on the bank of a river. "One who listened was a woman named Lydia, a dealer in purple goods from the town of Thyatira. She already reverenced God, and the Lord opened her heart to accept what Paul was saying. After she and her household had been baptized, she extended us an invitation: 'If you are convinced that I believe in the Lord, come and stay at my house.' She managed to prevail on us" (Acts 16:14-15).

However, it was not always so easy to find friends and collaborators of the gospel. The mission itself involved fatigue, fear, threats, suffering, misunderstanding, mistrust, and sometimes torture and imprisonment, or even death and martyrdom. Paul suffered these things when he and Silas were imprisoned and tortured but later was miraculously liberated (cf. Acts 16:19-40).

Lydia's house, however, became the center of the first missionary nucleus in Macedonia and perhaps in Europe as well. Later, Paul preached in Greece and in various parts of the civilized world. He encountered numerous obstacles and setbacks, but by the grace of God, his collaboration with Jesus, his courage and his missionary zeal, always prevailed (cf. Acts 17-20).

Here in a brief statement is a summation of the missionary spirit: "Both we ourselves and the people of Caesarea urged Paul not to proceed to Jerusalem. He answered with a question: 'Why are you crying and breaking my heart in this way? For the name of the Lord Jesus I am prepared, not only for imprisonment, but for death in Jerusalem.' Since he would not be dissuaded, we said nothing further except, 'The Lord's will be done'" (Acts 21:12-14).

The mission field for Paul was the entire world, since Jesus had told him in a vision: "Be on your way. I mean to send you far from here,

among the Gentiles" (Acts 22:21). Everywhere he proclaimed the gospel with great consistency and with much faith and love, courage and zeal. He founded many churches or local Christian communities. At the end he was imprisoned in Rome (cf. Acts 28:30-31) and eventually he was martyred for the faith in the year 67 A.D.

Every missionary is mindful of the command of Christ: "Go, therefore, and make disciples of all the nations. Baptize them in the name 'of the Father, and of the Son, and of the Holy Spirit.' Teach them to carry out everything I have commanded you. And know that I am with you always, until the end of the world" (Mt 28:19-20).

This mandate was addressed to the apostles and through them to the Church. Indeed, the vocation of every Christian is a missionary one: to bear witness to Christ, proclaiming salvation by one's life and works (cf. AA 3). Paul writes: "Preaching the gospel is not the subject of a boast; I am under compulsion and have no choice. I am ruined if I do not preach it! If I do it willingly, I have my recompense; if unwillingly, I am nonetheless entrusted with a charge" (1 Cor 9:16-17).

During the first three centuries of the Church's existence, Christianity encountered many difficulties, persecution and martyrdom. The Roman Empire fought against Christ and against the Church with all its power, but to no avail. In fact, because of the persecutions and the fidelity of the Christian faithful, the manifestation of the power of the Holy Spirit once again gave proof of his presence. Faith and love are stronger than hatred and death! So it was and still is in various parts of the world where the Church is bleeding but giving witness by living and proclaiming Christ.

The Second Vatican Council has stated: "The Church on earth is by its very nature missionary since, according to the plan of the Father, it has its origin in the mission of the Son and the Holy Spirit" (AG 2). "The Church . . . strives to preach the gospel to all men" (AG 1) "so that the power of the gospel may shine out in daily family and social life" (LG 35).

What does it mean to be a missionary today? It means to be a Christian wherever we are and wherever God calls us, through our example in daily life and at work. It means to have a sense of responsibility and full awareness, to have faith and love. The Second Vatican Council says: "In the present state of things which gives rise to a new situation for humankind, the Church, the salt of the earth and the light of the world, is even more urgently called upon to save and renew every creature, so that all things might be restored in Christ, and so that in him men might form one family and one people of God" (AG 1).

The missionary character of the faithful consists in "a profound interior renewal so that being vitally conscious of their responsibility for the spread of the gospel they might play their part in missionary work among the nations" (AG 35).

In the history of the Church there have been many outstanding missionaries in various parts of the world. To recall some of them: Augustine of Canterbury in England; Cyril and Methodius in the Slav world; Bartholomew de las Casas in Latin America; St. Isaac Jogues and companions in North America; St. Francis Xavier in India and Japan; Francis Capillas in China; and Daniel Comboni in Africa.

Undoubtedly, the best-known missionary of our times was Mother Teresa of Calcutta. What did she think about the missions?

The specific purpose of our Congregation is the conversion and sanctification of the poor who live in the slums or in colonies of outcasts; that is, to assist the sick and the dying, to care for the street children, to visit the beggars . . . to work for the conversion and salvation of the poor. . . . To convert and sanctify is God's work. . . . To bring the light of Christ to the darkness of the hovels in the slums, we must bring our Lord where he has never gone before. . . .

The surest means for preaching Christianity to the pagans is our joy, our happiness. Here is one example from my own life. Once a man entered Kalighat. I was there too. After a while he turned to me and said: "I came here with great hatred in my heart for God and for people. I came here empty, without faith, embittered; but when I saw a Sister giving careful attention to a patient, and she did it with joy, I realized that God still loves. I am changed. I believe that God exists and he still loves. . . ."

When we opened Baroda, a group of Hindus came to me and said: "Have you come to convert us?" I looked at them, smiled and said: "Of course; this is the treasure that I have. I would be pleased if all of you became Christians voluntarily, but I do not have the power or the desire to force anyone. Not even God can force anyone who does not wish it. . . ."

Goodness has converted more persons than zeal, knowledge or eloquence. . . . If we want the poor to see Christ in us, we must first see Christ in them. (Mother Teresa)

Many missionaries have gone off to the missions to convert others. They have built schools and hospitals and have performed many works of charity. Mother Teresa started from a very different basic concept: to love and serve God in every suffering person. Consequently, none of Mother Teresa's programs or projects are "catholic"; they are for everyone. She knew that it is only by giving witness that one can change people's hearts. This evangelical strategy is truly a new and original missionary effort in which the person is the challenge to our faith, love and service.

Mother Teresa explained it this way:

It is very difficult, if not impossible, to give Jesus to others if we do not already have him in our hearts. . . . To "convert" is to bring to God. To "sanctify" is to fill with God. To convert and sanctify are works of God. Our work is to love, to bear witness to God who is love. . . . We do not try to impose our faith on others. We only try to act in such a way that Christ will infuse his light and life in us and, through us, into the world of suffering. . . . Nationality means nothing in the rules of our Constitutions . . . and for that reason we must never have an unfavorable attitude toward those of another nationality or religion.

Evangelization is at the service of God and the whole person. The Church has always respected the various peoples' languages, cultures, traditions and religions. Paul did the same so as to bring people to Christ. This is still a valid method, because it is the one Christ used. He became incarnate in a particular environment, language, culture and people but was not limited to that; he worked for the salvation of all.

The laity's participation in missionary work, besides being based on solid theological principles, is particularly necessary today. This follows logically from the scarcity of vocations to the clerical and religious life, the population increase in many missionary countries, scientific and technological advances, and the absence of religious liberty in some countries. Consequently, it becomes ever more evident that to be a Christian is to be a missionary here and now, wherever we may be.

We must never be afraid to proclaim the good news in any environment. I notice that people today have a greater hunger for God than they did yesterday. Previously there was a great deal of external religiosity, but now there is in many persons a desire to find God in the interior of their heart. This is the reason why especially today we should be bearers and proclaimers of Christ. . . .

In India we have an ever greater number of Hindus, Muslims, Buddhists who take part in our work. Why do they come to us? Because they sense the presence of God; they want to serve God in their way, and they realize that with prayer and sacrifice they can really do so. (Mother Teresa)

Baptism: Spiritual Rebirth

I solemnly assure you, no one can enter into God's kingdom without being begotten of water and Spirit.

John 3:5

Besides bodily life, God has given us spiritual and supernatural life through the sacrament of baptism, because he has introduced us into his great family of the Church. . . . What a beautiful gift is baptism, through which we become children of God, members of his Mystical Body, the Church, and heirs of eternal life.

Mother Teresa

Baptism is the sacrament of faith, our spiritual rebirth. It is one of the sacraments of Christian initiation, together with confirmation and the eucharist. Without faith, salvation is impossible, and therefore there is a close relationship between faith and baptism, which opens the doors to the other sacraments.

Faith and baptism are one and the same thing, in the sense that by believing the person who is baptized receives the fruits of salvation and becomes a member of the community of believers which is the Church. Through faith a person is capable of finding, living and loving God and of enjoying intimate union with him even now in Jesus Christ. Consequently, the reception of baptism is not a leap in the dark, an uncertain step; it is the divine dynamism which gives us supernatural life, makes us children of God and members of the Church, through which we have known this new life.

The Church teaches us that baptism is the sacrament of spiritual renewal, of forgiveness of sins through water and the Holy Spirit. And we should mention here the active and dynamic nature of baptism, not only as an action already performed and completed, but also as an insertion of the person into divine life. For this reason baptism justifies us through the merits of Jesus Christ; it bestows on us the baptismal grace of supernatural life, together with the virtues of faith, hope and charity. These are the supernatural powers that constitute a complete orientation of life to Life.

The sacrament was already prefigured in the Old Testament, in the description of creation, when "darkness covered the abyss, while a mighty wind [the Spirit of God] swept over the waters" (Gn 1:2). Baptism was also prefigured in Noah's ark, in which he and his family were saved (cf. Gn 6), and in the passage through the Red Sea and the escape from slavery in Egypt (cf. Ex 14:10-31).

Jesus Christ is the fulfillment of the ancient promises, of all people's desire for peace, freedom, justice, and love. Through him can each one of us be and live as a child of God. Jesus himself received a baptism at the hands of John the Baptist, at which time his nature and mission were revealed: "Suddenly the sky opened and he saw the Spirit of God descend like a dove and hover over him. With that, a voice from the heavens said, 'This is my beloved Son. My favor rests on him'" (Mt 3:16-17). Later on, water and blood flowed from the pierced side of the crucified Christ (cf. Jn 19:34), and this has traditionally been interpreted as symbols of the sacraments of baptism and the eucharist.

With great sacrifice and love, Jesus fulfilled the mission given to him by his Father, and then he entrusted it to his apostles, saying: "Full authority has been given to me both in heaven and on earth; go, therefore, and make disciples of all the nations. Baptize them in the name 'of the Father, and of the Son, and of the Holy Spirit.' Teach them to carry out everything I have commanded you" (Mt 28:18-19).

Jesus also emphasized the importance of the sacrament of baptism: "Go into the whole world and proclaim the good news to all creation. The man who believes in it and accepts baptism will be saved; the man who refuses to believe in it will be condemned" (Mk 16:16).

Paul speaks of the effects of baptism in this way: "Each one of you is a son of God because of your faith in Christ Jesus. All of you who have been baptized into Christ have clothed yourselves with him. There does not exist among you Jew or Greek, slave or freeman, male or female. All are one in Christ Jesus. Furthermore, if you belong to Christ you are the descendants of Abraham, which means you inherit all that was promised" (Gal 3:26-29).

The Second Vatican Council teaches: "Incorporated into the Church by baptism, the faithful are appointed by their baptismal character to Christian religious worship; reborn as sons of God, they must profess before men the faith they have received from God through the Church" (LG 11).

Faith and baptism are one gift not only for us, but also for others; they constitute one and the same mission: "All Christians by the example of their lives and the witness of the word, wherever they live, have an obligation to manifest the new man which they put on in baptism" (AG 11).

Today some people ask: If baptism confers a new life and mission, why should infants be baptized? They are not yet able to accept the gift of faith and salvation, to live for Jesus Christ. The Church's answer is simple and convincing: The ability to live for Christ is born of the faith of God's people. By placing infants into this same ambit of faith, we assure them a Christian education and formation from the beginning of their lives.

Today as always, the fundamental question

is not the baptism of the newborn, but the existence and efficacy of faith in the family, in the community, and in the Church. They must assume the responsibility of nurturing the faith of the newly baptized within the community. Thus the history of salvation is made present through the Church and through the life of the sacraments. The Church is celebrating salvation when it baptizes because it is gathering the fruits of the redeeming death and resurrection of Christ. Thus the Church spiritually gives birth to its members, but the Church itself is also generated from the same life that is in Christ Jesus.

From a divine point of view, salvation has already been accomplished and it is given to us through Jesus Christ and his Church. But from our human point of view, salvation is something yet to be accomplished, a mission to be carried forward, a plan to be fulfilled. Here lies the dynamism of the Christian life, expressed in theology with the concepts of "already" and "not yet": it is already accomplished on God's part but not yet fulfilled on ours.

Paul explains this truth as follows: "He saved us; not because of any righteous deeds we had done, but because of his mercy. He saved us through the baptism of new birth and renewal by the Holy Spirit" (Tt 3:5).

Mother Teresa said:

I think that no one has given us more than God, who has given us everything freely. . . . We thank God that he has given us his Son Jesus, so that he could be born into the world as we were and should be like us in everything except sin. God has thus manifested the greatness and beauty of human life by becoming man himself. . . .

Jesus says in the gospel: "Unless you become like these little ones, you shall not enter the kingdom of heaven." And what does it mean to be little? It means to have a cleansed heart, a pure heart, a heart that possesses Jesus who is in my heart, to live the grace of baptism in faith, hope and charity. . . . Jesus loves us, always and everywhere.

Confirmation: Strengthened in the Holy Spirit

*You did not receive a spirit of slavery
leading you back into fear,
but a spirit of adoption
through which we cry out,
"Abba!" (that is, "Father").*
Romans 8:15

*Our Lady is the masterpiece of the Holy
Spirit, who descended upon her
at the annunciation, after her fiat.
She conceived Jesus through the power
of the Holy Spirit, and she followed him
faithfully until her death. . . .
She collaborated with the Holy Spirit
in attaining perfection and also with great
love in the life of the early Church.
Together with the apostles
in common prayer, she prepared
for and received the Holy Spirit.*
Mother Teresa

The second sacrament of Christian initiation is confirmation or chrismation. It is called confirmation because it confirms or strengthens the grace received in baptism, and for this reason some call it a "second baptism." This sacrament disposes us for greater responsibility and maturity in the faith as well as a for greater commitment as a witness and an apostle.

"By the sacrament of confirmation [the faithful] are more perfectly bound to the Church and are endowed with the special strength of the Holy Spirit. Hence they are, as true witnesses of Christ, strictly obliged to spread the faith by word and deed" (LG 11; cf. LG 33).

Jesus also confirms the presence of the Holy Spirit in us in his life and mission: "The Spirit of the Lord is upon me; therefore he has anointed me. He has sent me to bring glad tidings to the poor, to proclaim liberty to captives, recovery of sight to the blind and release to prisoners, to announce a year of favor from the Lord" (Lk 4:18-19). Jesus then presented himself to the people in these words: "Today this scripture passage is fulfilled in your hearing" (Lk 4:21). The Holy Spirit was also manifested at the baptism of Jesus in the Jordan and throughout his public life.

The Holy Spirit was the primary protagonist in the early Church, and he has continued in that role through the centuries. Hence the early Christians, besides being baptized, were anointed and received the Holy Spirit in confirmation: "[Peter and John] upon arriving imposed hands on them, and they received the Holy Spirit" (Acts 8:17).

Initially, baptism and confirmation were received at the same time and Cyprian referred to this as "the double sacrament." Later, the two were separated for pastoral reasons, and special importance was given to confirmation by being administered by the bishop. This began as early as the third century, although it is not found in the Ordo Romanus until the seventh century.

Thomas Aquinas (1225-74) wrote as follows: "Baptism and confirmation are like birth and growth; in confirmation one reaches the fulfillment or realization of baptism." However, in the Orthodox Church and in the Catholic churches of the eastern rite, the sacraments of baptism and confirmation (chrismation) are conferred at the same time.

There are two external signs in the conferral of confirmation: the anointing with oil of chrism and the imposition of hands by the bishop, signifying the reception of the Holy Spirit.

Jesus fulfilled after his resurrection what he had promised the apostles: "'As the Father has sent me, so I send you.' Then he breathed on them and said: 'Receive the Holy Spirit. If you forgive men's sins, they are forgiven them; if you hold them bound, they are held bound'" (Jn 20:21-23).

The Church was born of the Holy Spirit and lives by the Holy Spirit, who carries on the work of Jesus. Under the inspiration of the Holy Spirit, the apostles gave testimony to the resurrection of Christ, as Jesus had promised:

"I will ask the Father and he will give you another Paraclete—to be with you always: The Spirit of truth, whom the world cannot accept, since it neither sees him nor recognizes him; but you can recognize him because he remains with you and will be within you" (Jn 14:16-17).

This was realized on the feast of Pentecost, again as Jesus had promised: "The Paraclete, the Holy Spirit, whom my Father will send in my name, will instruct you in everything, and remind you of all that I told you" (Jn 14:26).

Paul lists the fruits of the presence of the Holy Spirit as "love, joy, peace, patient endurance, kindness, generosity, faith, mildness and chastity" (Gal 5:22). In the Creed we profess: "We believe in the Holy Spirit, the Lord, the giver of life, who proceeds from the Father and the Son. With the Father and the Son he is worshiped and glorified. He has spoken through the prophets" (CCC, p. 50).

To remain faithful to Christ and to be able to proclaim his message, the Church has need of the Holy Spirit (cf. Acts 4:30; 5:42; 6:7; 9:20). He is present today in his Mystical Body, the Church, to carry on the work of salvation "even to the ends of the earth" (Acts 1:8).

Our Lady is the model of obedience and collaboration in the work of the Holy Spirit, because at every moment of her life she was a prompt and active cooperator in the work of redemption.

We too have need of the Holy Spirit in order to be authentic Christians in our life and in our work. The Second Vatican Council says: "All Christians by the example of their life and the witness of their word, wherever they live, have an obligation to manifest the new man which they put on in baptism, and to reveal the power of the Holy Spirit by whom they were strengthened at confirmation, so that others, seeing their good works, might glorify the Father and more perfectly perceive the true meaning of human life and the universal solidarity of mankind" (AG 11).

The first Christians died for Christ, guided and sustained by the Holy Spirit. They were recognized from the fact that they loved one another. The world has never had such a need for love as it has today. For that reason we have great need of the Holy Spirit, to teach us how to receive, live, and love Jesus in our neighbor. . . . To cooperate well with the Holy Spirit we also need silence, prayer, and meditation, as Mary practiced them. . . . Let us pray each day with the Church: "Come, Holy Spirit; renew the face of the earth," our hearts, ourselves, and the whole world. The real "motor" of our spiritual life, of our conversion, is the Holy Spirit. (Mother Teresa)

The Eucharist: Life of the Church

The third sacrament of initiation is the eucharist, the presence of Jesus in us and for us under the appearance of the consecrated bread and wine. This constitutes the greatest treasure of the Church, the universal offering of God's love for us, divine life. Many titles are used to designate the eucharist: the Lord's supper (cf. 1 Cor 11:20); the table of the Lord (cf. 1 Cor 10:21); the breaking of the bread (cf. Acts 2:42); or the synaxis, the Mass, the holy sacrifice, the eucharist, the liturgy. In order to remain with us always, Jesus instituted this sacrament of the eucharist and also, at the Last Supper, the sacrament of the holy order of the priesthood of the New Testament.

On two occasions the disciples did not understand clearly Jesus' message: When he predicted his death (cf. Mt 16:21-23) and when he spoke about the eucharist (cf. Jn 6:32-58). Others walked away, saying: "This sort of talk is hard to endure! How can anyone take it seriously?" (Jn 6:60).

We too are faced with the mystery of faith which we proclaim at every Mass immediately after the consecration. We cannot fully comprehend it; it is only with faith and love that we can accept it, love it, and live it. That is what Peter did in his name and in the name of the other apostles and ourselves. When Jesus asked the apostles: "Do you want to leave me too?"

Peter responded: "Lord, to whom shall we go? You have the words of eternal life. We have come to believe; we are convinced that you are God's holy one" (Jn 6:67-69). This was a response of faith (we have believed), a response of love (to whom shall we go?), and a response of life (you have the words of eternal life).

Oh, what more could my Jesus do but give me his flesh as food? No, not even God could do more or show me a love greater than this intimate union of Jesus with our soul and with our body. The saints understood this very well, and they would spend hours in preparation and then more time in thanksgiving. (Mother Teresa)

The Last Supper was celebrated in the context of the paschal mystery and the passion of Christ (cf. Mt 14:22-26; 26:17-19; Lk 22:7-13). It was also celebrated in the context of the Chosen People, as the starting point of the history of salvation. The connection between the paschal lamb and Jesus is evident. He will be sacrificed on the cross. The miracle of his love is this: the changing of bread and wine into his body and blood (cf. Mt 26:26-29; Mk 14:22-25; Lk 22:15-20; 1 Cor 11:23-25). Then Jesus concludes with this marvelous statement: "Do this as a remembrance of me" (Lk 22:19). The apostles gratefully accepted this gift of love, and they continued to celebrate the eucharist in the midst of the Christian community (cf. Acts 2:42-46).

The Second Vatican Council describes the eucharist as "the source and summit of the Christian life" in which "they offer the divine victim to God and themselves along with it" (LG 11). Consequently, the eucharist is not simply a remembrance; it is a real actuation of the presence of Christ in our midst. The Church celebrates the eucharist not simply as a memorial service, but it makes Christ present and active at every moment and place where Mass is celebrated. Activating as it does the death and resurrection of Christ, it also produces all the fruits of salvation.

"To accomplish so great a work Christ is always present in his Church, especially in her liturgical celebrations. He is present in the sacrifice of the Mass not only in the person of his minister, 'the same now offering, through the ministry of priests, who formerly offered himself on the cross,' but especially in the eucharistic species" (SC 7).

During the eucharistic celebration God addresses his word to us, his message for our life, and he does so through the scriptural readings and the preaching of the Church. We offer bread and wine, the fruit of human labor and the fruit of the vine, and God transforms it into his body and blood, thereby giving himself to us as a gift. We are nourished by his body and blood when we receive communion, which strengthens our union with God and with the community.

In the celebration of the eucharist the Church declares: "We recall Christ's death, his descent among the dead, his resurrection, and his ascension to your right hand; and, looking forward to his coming in glory, we offer you his body and blood, the acceptable sacrifice which brings salvation to the whole world" (Eucharistic Prayer IV; cf. 1 Cor 11:25-26).

The eucharist is the bread of faith, hope and charity and of unity. Augustine said: "O sacrament of piety; O sacrament of unity; O sacrament of love." The eucharist is truly a mystery of faith (cf. 1 Tm 3:9), a gift of Christ's love, the perpetual activation of salvation, the prolongation of Christ's real presence and love for the world.

The Church exists, grows and makes progress because Jesus nourishes it (cf. LG 26) and the Holy Spirit guides and protects it. Only through faith can we discover, love and live this tremendous mystery. In the eucharist Jesus nourishes and actuates the totality of our faith. Hence, the Second Vatican Council has stated: "No Christian community is built up which does not grow from and hinge on the celebration of the most holy eucharist" (PO 6). According to Augustine, the eucharist is "the banquet of the Lord and the unity of the body of Christ." The eucharist is the inexhaustible and eternal font of life and love, the viaticum of salvation, medicine for sin and the pledge of eternity.

The mission of the Church has been defined by the Second Vatican Council in terms of the eucharist: "Christ left to his followers a pledge of this hope and food for the journey in the sacrament of faith, in which natural elements, the fruits of man's cultivation, are changed into his glorified body and blood, as a supper of brotherly fellowship and a foretaste of the heavenly banquet" (GS 35).

The eucharist is the new Pasch, our Pasch, in which Christ offers himself to the Father and gives himself to us as food and nourishment. In receiving communion, we must not only open our mouths, but especially our hearts and ourselves to God's presence. In this way we can become living tabernacles of his presence and love in the world.

Jesus said: "I myself am the living bread come down from heaven. If anyone eats this bread he shall live forever; the bread I will give

is my flesh, for the life of the world. . . . He who feeds on my flesh and drinks my blood has life eternal, and I will raise him up on the last day. . . . The man who feeds on my flesh and drinks my blood remains in me, and I in him" (Jn 6:51-56, passim).

And Paul writes: "I received from the Lord what I handed on to you, namely, that the Lord Jesus on the night in which he was betrayed took bread, and after he had given thanks, broke it and said, 'This is my body, which is for you. Do this in remembrance of me'" (1 Cor 11:23-24).

Mother Teresa spoke of the power of the eucharist in this way:

In our hearts let us adore Jesus, who spent thirty of his thirty-three years in silence and began his public life with forty days of silence. . . . Let us adore Jesus in the silence of the eucharist. . . . People do not hunger for us. They hunger for God. They hunger for Jesus in the eucharist. He gives us himself in the eucharist and invites us to grow in his love. Christ's love for us gives us strength and prompts us to give ourselves for him. . . . In this way we make Jesus present in the world today. We cannot separate our life from the eucharist. . . . People ask: "Where do the Sisters get the joy and energy to do all that they do?" The eucharist should be at the center of our life. Ask Jesus to remain with you, to work with you, so that you can transform your work into prayer. . . . The eucharist is so small, but it produces great effects, because it is the bread of life and of love. Without Jesus I would not be able to live my life for a single day or a single hour.

In our Congregation it was the custom to

have an hour of adoration each week, and then, in 1973, we decided to have an hour of adoration each day. Since we started to have our daily hour of adoration, our love for Jesus has become more intense, our love for one another is more comprehensive, our love for the poor is more compassionate, and we have doubled the number of vocations. God has blessed us with many wonderful vocations.

When I visited Mother Teresa in the hospital in Calcutta in 1989, immediately after greeting me, she said:

First adore the Lord in the tabernacle; then come and we shall talk.

And there on a little table was Jesus in the tabernacle. Later she told me:

Only now do I understand the reason for my illness, and I am quite content. See, I am in good company with Jesus. All for Jesus.

Afterward, she spoke to me about future projects, the telegram she had sent to the governor of Albania, the letters and telegrams she sent each day to various parts of the world. Then, before I left, she confided to me with great emotion and conviction:

You will see; soon I shall bring Jesus to Albania also.

And that is precisely what happened. She was the first dove of peace to enter suffering Albania. That was in August of 1990. And now there are seven houses of the Missionaries of Charity, numerous vocations, and a fruitful apostolate. So Jesus has returned again to Albania, thanks to our Mother Teresa!

"We cannot separate our life from the eucharist"

The Church Cares for the Sick

With that they went off, preaching the need of repentance. They expelled many demons, anointed the sick with oil, and worked many cures.

Mark 6:12-13

Today the passion of Christ is renewed in the life of those who suffer, who are sick, poor, and abandoned. To accept suffering is a gift from God; it is a sign of the maturity of our faith, the holiness of our life.

Mother Teresa

Jesus met sick people in many circumstances. Some he miraculously cured, while to others he spoke words of comfort. To all he showed understanding and love. Sickness is present in various stages of life. The sick suffer in the body from pain and discomfort and in the soul from forced inactivity and the inability to engage in productive work. They are often a burden to themselves and feel like they are one to others.

Sickness can be the most difficult trial in a person's life, causing fear and anguish. Even the healthy person, seeing others suffer, might ask: How long will my health last? Medical science and research have made great progress and prolonged life, but they have not resolved the fundamental question of life: Why am I living? From whence do I come and where am I going? Why must I suffer and ultimately die?

Unfortunately, the sick person today is often marginalized. Think of the number of persons in hospital beds who are anonymous and alone, just another case in the medical records. So many people today have a fear of life and of death. Fear of life, because there are so many ways in which it can be destroyed. Even the unborn infant can be murdered by abortion or deprived of life by artificial contraception. Fear of death, which prompts society to marginalize the old, the sick and the inmates of institutions, keeping them far removed from everyone else. Modern people want to accept only the better part of life, such as youth and maturity, which are the active and productive stages of life. They seem to forget that just as there is no youth or maturity without infancy, so also the human person inevitably ages and marches on toward death and eternity.

Modern culture is basically anti-life; it rejects life at various levels of human existence. This leads to the logical conclusion that the most important thing is to have good health. On the other hand, sickness gives us a chance to get to know ourselves and to recognize our limitations. As we lie suffering in bed, we learn to appreciate life more, even as a mortal illness directs us toward the transcendent. For we realize that no one can help us or save us from the inevitable.

You who are incurably sick can do much for the poor, because each day you experience the crucifixion together with Jesus. By your prayer you irrigate our labor, and you help us to offer to others the strength to work. . . . You suffer and we labor. . . . Together we hold the same chalice; we carry the same cross.

There are medications for every type of sickness. But if there are not good hands to serve and generous hearts to love, I think it is impossible ever to cure the terrible sickness of not feeling that one is loved. (Mother Teresa)

If a Christian community exists, there is also a sense of sharing in good and evil. Even in the Old Testament, where sickness was seen as a punishment from God for sin, care of the sick was considered a work of mercy. The Church, following the teaching of Christ, continues the care of the sick and cures many (cf. Acts 28:8-9). Jesus had told the apostles: "As you go, make this announcement: 'The reign of God is at hand!' Cure the sick, raise the dead, heal the leprous, expel demons. The gift you have received, give as a gift" (Mt 10:7-8).

In ancient times oil was one of the most common medications. It could be swallowed for medicinal purposes or used as a lotion for massage, as a cosmetic for beauty, or as a salve for wounds. It was also used by the Jews in religious ceremonies for the consecration of religious objects (cf. Gn 28:18; Lv 10-12) or for the investiture of kings (cf. Ex 29:7) or prophets (cf. 1 K 19:16). The anointed one par excellence, of course, is Jesus, the Son of God, the Messiah, the Savior.

The sacrament of anointing is referred to in the Letter of James: "Is there anyone sick among you? He should ask for the presbyters of the Church. They in turn are to pray over him, anointing him with oil in the Name [of the Lord]. This prayer uttered in faith will reclaim the one who is ill, and the Lord will restore him to health. If he has committed any sins, forgiveness will be his" (Jas 5:14-15). The effects of the sacrament are not from the oil but from faith. The Lord stands behind the prayers of the priests to heal and to pardon.

The Council of Trent defined the anointing of the sick as a sacrament instituted by Christ. It is administered by a priest with oil blessed by the bishop, and with prayer and the laying on of hands. The Council then stated that this sacrament is to be received especially when in danger of death.

The Second Vatican Council stated that the anointing of the sick "is not a sacrament for those only who are at the point of death. Hence, as soon as anyone of the faithful begins to be in danger of death from sickness or old age, the fitting time for him to receive this sacrament has certainly already arrived" (SC 73; cf. CCC, 1514).

Moreover, the Second Vatican Council has restored to this sacrament the community aspect, since the anointing pertains not only to the sick or the priest, but to the Church. We are all members of the same body of Christ (cf. 1 Cor 12:25). This means that sickness, healing, and death are not strictly individual acts or events; they are communal, as is everything else in human life.

Moreover, the time of sickness is a good occasion for the believer to unite himself with the sufferings of Christ. The revised rite for the anointing of the sick states that "only the mystery of the death and resurrection of Christ can redeem and save our mortal life." Hence, the Second Vatican Council has stated: "By the sacred anointing of the sick and the prayer of the priests the whole Church commends those who are ill to the suffering and glorified Lord that he may raise them up and save them. And indeed she exhorts them to contribute to the good of the people of God by freely uniting themselves to the passion and death of Christ" (LG 11).

God has given me a great gift—strong and robust health—although I may appear weak. . . . But in time of sickness, especially that of 1989, when my heart played jokes, I have reflected on sickness and the sick. . . . I now have "two hearts": My natural heart, which is Albanian, and an artificial heart, which is American (my pacemaker). While I was sick I received the anointing of the sick, and I was nourished with Christ every day. For me, to die and go to the Father is a great day that I am waiting for, the feast day on which I shall be united with my Lord, meet my family and many beloved persons. (Mother Teresa)

Then, she wrote to the Sisters who care for the sick:

When we are caring for the sick and the needy, we are touching the body of the suffering Christ, and this touch makes us heroic; it helps us overcome the repugnance and the natural reaction that is in all of us. This is the eye of faith and of love, to see Christ in the sick and to serve him, sharing their suffering, everything. . . . Suffering is not a punishment. Jesus does not punish. Suffering is a sign, a sign that God loves us. . . . Through suffering, pain, the cross, sickness, and death, we arrive at life, at the resurrection. (Mother Teresa)

The Church: Community of Reconciliation

Receive the Holy Spirit.
If you forgive men's sins,
they are forgiven them;
if you hold them bound,
they are held bound.
(John 20:22-23)

Only one thing is indispensable for us:
confession. This is nothing else
but an act of humility. We call it
"the sacrament of penance,"
but it is really a sacrament of love,
a sacrament of pardon. . . .
It is a place where I let Jesus
remove from me everything
that can divide and destroy.
In confession we should be very simple,
like children.
Mother Teresa

The entire redemptive work of Jesus is to free us from the slavery of sin and death. His care for the whole person, body and soul, like a doctor and friend of humanity, was constant. That's why he worked so many miracles and healings. On one occasion he said: "My son, your sins are forgiven" (Mk 2:5); and then he healed the body: "I command you: Stand up! Pick up your mat, and walk again" (Mk 2:11). These two actions represent two distinct sacraments: the sacrament of reconciliation, formerly called penance or confession, and the anointing of the sick, which asks for bodily healing. The New Testament has numerous references to the sacrament of reconciliation:

"Many who had become believers came forward and openly confessed their former practices" (Acts 19:18).

"If we acknowledge our sins, he who is just can be trusted to forgive our sins and cleanse us from every wrong" (1 Jn 1:9).

"Declare your sins to one another, and pray for one another, that you may find healing" (Jas 5:16).

The Council of Trent defined confession as a sacrament instituted by Christ for the forgiveness of sins committed after baptism. The same Council stipulated the three conditions required for forgiveness:

— sorrow for sins committed;

— confession of sins committed;

— satisfaction for sins committed, to be given by the priest in the name of the Church as a penance for one's sins.

The Second Vatican Council speaks of sin in a biblical context, as a rejection of God and his love. Hence the need for reconciliation as an act of love, a return to God through the community of the Church. This is a sacrament of pardon.

It is necessary to go to the root of the evil of sin. Sin is always the experience of abandoning the Father's house, the refusal to act like and to be a son (cf. Lk 15:12-13). Sin distances a person from God and also from the community of salvation which is the Church. In this sacrament the faithful receive pardon through the mercy of God and the instrumentality of the Church. They need to be reconciled to God and to the Church and their neighbor, because by their sin they have inflicted a wound (cf. LG 11).

True conversion means to love God and, out of that love, to hate sin and slavery to sin. Then, "those who approach the sacrament of penance obtain pardon from God's mercy for the offense committed against him and are, at the same time, reconciled with the Church, which they have wounded by their sins and which by charity, by example and by prayer labors for their conversion" (LG 11). Unfortunately, many Christians have lost the meaning of faith as life with God. They have also lost a sense of sin and can no longer appreciate the relationship between God, our life, our actions, and sin. Many others have not lost the sense of faith, but they live only for themselves; they no longer appreciate the ecclesial or community dimension of faith. For them, sin is a strictly private and personal affair.

When one no longer appreciates the filial bond between humanity and God, sin is no longer seen as a rejection of God. When one no longer admits the connection between sin, the sinner, and the Christian community, he or she logically rejects the figure of the confessor as representative of God and the Christian community. This accounts for the unfortunate crisis today in the sacrament of reconciliation; two essential elements are missing from the lives of many believers: God and the Church. In the "New Order of Penance" the Church is trying to restore the sense of God and of community through the word of God: "It is right that the sacrament of penance should begin with the hearing of the word of God: Through his word God calls men to repentance and leads them to true change of heart" (MS 24).

At the same time, the sense of guilt for sin remains with us. How can we escape from this situation? By entrusting ourselves completely to Christ, with great faith and love: the faith of the Church and in the Church and in the sacrament of pardon. But God has to take the initiative.

How beautiful it is to receive pardon from God, who will never refuse it if we ask for it with faith and love. We also need to learn to pardon others, thus bearing witness to God's pardon and goodness. His alone is the power that can change us and make us better, thereby leading us along the path to sanctity and salvation. God is always offering us his love and pardon; we should also offer love and pardon to others. A person of faith never despairs and never judges or condemns others.

When we realize that we are sinners and are in need of forgiveness, it will be much easier for us to pardon others. Until I understand this, it will cost me a great deal to say "I forgive you" to anyone who asks me. It is not necessary to be a Christian in order to forgive. Whatever our belief, we should learn how to forgive if we want to love truly. (Mother Teresa)

It is difficult to accept our inability to fulfill our desires and projects, to admit that we need others to satisfy our needs. And if the inability is absolute, as when a loved one has an incurable sickness, a friendship which seemed eternal is falling apart, a love is ending and there is nothing we can do, we become painfully aware of our limitations and helplessness.

Something similar to this we experience when we are faced with the reality of sin, when we discover our weaknesses, our defects, our internal wounds. The desire to change and to improve is then very strong. But perhaps the possibilities are few, very few. Then we feel trapped, with no hope of escape.

What can be done? We can submit completely to circumstances, and our life will become a game of fatalism. Or we can look for a solution outside ourselves. The awareness of our own limitations, which we acquire through sin, can become the link that connects us with the divine omnipotence. If we are certain about divine love, then sin becomes an occasion for the merciful intervention of the Lord.

The key to change and conversion is Jesus. We can abandon ourselves completely to him, because he alone has conquered the world, sin, death, and the devil. And the best occasion that God offers us for change and conversion is in confession. To confess one's sins is not simply to lament the past, to make an exact examination of conscience, to identify our desires and deeds, and then to make some act of humility before God. Confession involves all these things, but it is above all an encounter with Jesus in order to open the doors to a better tomorrow. Consequently, the sacrament of reconciliation does not look only to the past; it is also a preparation for and a pledge of the future. It gives us pardon, love, and confidence. It is the firm basis for a new life and for becoming a different person in a different world.

Only one thing is indispensable: confession. This is nothing else but an act of humility. We call it the sacrament of penance, through which God gives us his pardon and love as a guaranty of change. (Mother Teresa)

If sin is essentially a rejection of the love of God, confession is an act of accepting his love, which is always greater than our sin. The change of our life is not our work but God's. This is a profound truth of our faith and one of the best proofs that Jesus is alive and operative in the world. What is impossible for human beings, namely, to change oneself or others, is possible for God. We should believe this and try to make it possible for ourselves and for others by opening ourselves to God and cooperating with our neighbor.

The Christian must learn to pardon in order to receive pardon. Without pardon and love there is no life. . . .

Confession strengthens the soul, because a confession well made—the confession of a sinful son returning to the Father—always generates humility, and humility is strength. . . . The subject matter should be my sins, my sorrow, and pardon: how to overcome temptation; how to practice virtue; how to increase my love of God. . . .

The sacrament of penance is an act of perfect love of God for humanity and for the entire universe. It seeks to reconcile us with God, among ourselves, and with God's creation. It fosters unity in Christ, with Christ and through Christ of everything that was destroyed by sin. It is for us a joyful identification with Christ crucified. . . . We should be able to distinguish between self-knowledge and sin. To know oneself will help one to rise again, while sin and weakness cause one to fall again and to feel discouraged. Therefore, turn to Jesus so that he will sustain you in your weakness, but if you think that you are strong, you will not think that you need the Lord. . . .

Have no fear. God loves us and wants us to love one another as he loves us. Needy, weak, and sinners that we are, he loves us with an infinitely faithful love. (Mother Teresa)

The Priesthood:
Serving God and Humanity

The harvest is good
but laborers are scarce.
Beg the harvest master
to send out laborers to gather his harvest.
Matthew 9:37-38

A vocation
is only a call to belong entirely to Christ,
with the conviction that nothing
can separate me from his love.
A vocation
is an invitation to be in love with God
and to manifest that love.
Mother Teresa

Jesus Christ is the only true mediator. In his paschal mystery he is priest, victim, sacrifice and salvation. He came to serve (cf. Mk 16:45; Mt 20:28) and to give his life for the world.

The ordained priest is a minister of Christ and of the Church. He serves God, the human person, and the community to bring redemption to all. By the three sacraments of initiation—baptism, confirmation and eucharist—we have all been called to sanctification, to perfection, to Christian life and witness; in a word, to salvation.

With the sacraments of priesthood and matrimony we have a choice of vocation and mission; we choose the way to carry out our common Christian calling. Through the priesthood Christ makes us participants of the sacramental life. "The Church, by celebrating the eucharist and by other means, especially the celebration of the divine office, is ceaselessly engaged in praising the Lord and interceding for the salvation of the entire world" (SC 83).

The priesthood of the Old Testament was conferred on the tribe of Levi and was entrusted with the service of offerings and sacrifice in the temple at Jerusalem and among the Chosen People. Everything that was prefigured in the Old Testament was realized in the New Testament in Jesus Christ. "God is one. One also is the mediator between God and men, the man Christ Jesus, who gave himself as a ransom for all" (1 Tm 2:5-6).

Jesus was "designated by God as high priest according to the order of Melchizedek" (Heb 5:10); "by one offering he has forever perfected those who are being sanctified" (Heb 10:14). "Jesus, because he remains forever, has a priesthood which does not pass away. Therefore he is always able to save those who approach God through him, since he forever lives to make intercession for them" (Heb 7:24-25). Every priesthood is a sharing in the priesthood of Christ. He calls, as he did with the apostles and disciples and their successors.

According to the Council of Trent, the ministerial priesthood performs several types of service: It teaches the people the message of Christ and of the Church, and it guides and sanctifies the people of God. The Second Vatican Council says: "The ministerial priest, by the sacred power that he has, forms and rules the priestly people; in the person of Christ he effects the eucharistic sacrifice and offers it to God in the name of all the people" (LG 10).

— The priesthood teaches the people: "Go, therefore, and make disciples of all the nations. Baptize them in the name of 'the Father, and of the Son, and of the Holy Spirit.' Teach them to carry out everything I have commanded you" (Mt 28:19-20).

"Day after day, both in the temple and at home, they never stopped teaching and proclaiming the good news of Jesus the Messiah" (Acts 5:42).

The word of God becomes flesh during the day, in meditation, in holy communion, in *contemplation, in adoration, in silence. The word which is within you, give it to others. (Mother Teresa)*

—The priesthood guides the people of God: in the liturgy, in prayer, in faith. The bishop is the apostle of the local church; the ordained priests are his closest collaborators.

The people need holy priests who are truly second Christs in their life and example. (Mother Teresa)

— The priesthood sanctifies the people of God: "Priests are configured to Christ the priest . . . so that as co-workers with the episcopal order they may build up the body of Christ, the Church" (PO 12).

Holiness is not a privilege of the few; it is the duty of all believers, and especially of us consecrated persons. (Mother Teresa)

According to the teaching of Christ, the apostolic tradition, and the faith of the Catholic Church, the ministerial priesthood has three grades.

The apostles were the recipients of the mandate of Christ (cf. Mt 28:19-20), and they passed the same mission on to their successors by the laying on of hands (cf. 1 Tm 4:13-16). The Second Vatican Council teaches: "The apostles were careful to appoint successors in this hierarchically constituted society. . . . Amongst those various offices which have been exercised in the Church from the earliest times the chief place, according to the witness of tradition, is held by the function of those who, through their appointment to the dignity and responsibility of bishop, and in virtue consequently of the unbroken succession, going back to the beginning, are regarded as transmitters of the apostolic line" (LG 20).

Together, these form "a unique apostolic college" in which "the Roman Pontiff, Peter's successor, and the bishops, the successors of the apostles, are related with and united to one another" (LG 22).

The ministerial priest shares in and collaborates with the priesthood of Christ and the apostles. "Because it is joined with the episcopal order the office of priests shares in the authority by which Christ himself builds up and sanctifies and rules his body" (PO 2).

As regards deacons, the Second Vatican Council has stated: "The divinely instituted ecclesiastical ministry is exercised in different degrees by those who even from ancient times have been called bishops, priests, and deacons" (LG 28). The diaconate or service to the community is fully in keeping with the tradition of Christ and the Church. Thus, we read in the Acts of the Apostles: "The Twelve assembled the community of the disciples and said, 'It is not right for us to neglect the word of God in order to wait on tables. Look around your own number, brothers, for seven men acknowledged to be deeply spiritual and prudent, and we shall appoint them to this task. This will permit us to concentrate on prayer and the ministry of the word'" (Acts 6:2-4).

For many centuries the diaconate had lost its original meaning, having been reduced simply to a preparatory step to ordination to the priesthood. Since the Second Vatican Council the permanent diaconate has been restored and is available even to married men, although the temporary diaconate is still conferred on candidates for the ministerial priesthood.

"At a lower level of the hierarchy are to be found deacons, who receive the imposition of hands 'not unto the priesthood, but unto the ministry.' For, strengthened by sacramental grace they are dedicated to the people of God, in conjunction with the bishop and his body of priests, in the service of the liturgy, of the gospel, and of works of charity. It pertains to the office of deacon . . . to administer baptism solemnly, to be custodian and distributor of the eucharist, in the name of the Church to assist at and to bless marriages, to bring Viaticum to the dying, to read the sacred scripture to the faithful, to instruct and exhort the people, to preside over the worship and the prayer of the faithful, to administer sacramentals, and to officiate at funerals and burial services" (LG 29). The deacon may not, however, celebrate Mass or hear confessions.

Today the Catholic Church is facing the serious problem of scarcity of vocations to the priesthood. The problem is particularly serious in the wealthy countries of the First World and is aggravated by the widespread practice of birth control and abortion.

A vocation is a gift from the Lord. Christ said: "I have chosen you. . . ." Young people today are searching for something to which they can give all or nothing. . . . To "renounce" means to offer my free will, my judgment, my life in a manifestation of faith; it means to love. An active love calls for suffering. Jesus showed his love by dying on the cross for us. True love will cost us a great deal of sacrifice. . . .

I think that vocations are lacking today

because there is little prayer in the family; also because there is too much wealth, too much comfort, not only in families but also in religious life. . . .

The most important event that I have experienced in my life is my encounter with Christ. He is my support. . . . Our yes to God must be without reservation. (Mother Teresa)

To carry on the work of Christ, the Church needs authentic collaborators who, for the love of God and the Church, will dedicate themselves freely and completely to his service. This is a task for the community and for everybody. "The whole Christian people ought to be made aware that it is their duty to cooperate in their various ways, both by earnest prayer and by other means available to them, to ensure that the Church will always have those priests who are needed for the fulfillment of her divine mission. . . . In sermons, in catechetical instruction and in periodicals the needs of the Church, both local and universal, are to be made known clearly" (PO 11).

Jesus continues to invite, but it depends on the individual to accept or refuse the divine call. The words of Christ are always relevant, but especially today: "The harvest is good but laborers are scarce. Beg the harvest master to send out laborers to gather his harvest" (Mt 9:7-38).

Matrimony and Virginity

*"For this reason
a man shall leave his father and mother
and cling to his wife,
and the two shall become as one."
Thus, they are no longer two
but one flesh.
Therefore, let no man separate
what God has joined.*
Matthew 19:5-6

*By our vow of chastity
we renounce the natural gift
that God gave us to become mothers,
in exchange for a gift that is yet greater,
that of being virgins for Christ,
of sharing in a much more
sublime motherhood.*
Mother Teresa

We were created by God out of love and for love, as beings that tend toward union with God and communion with neighbor. This union-communion is realized in a special way in marriage, wherein a man and a woman join together in love to live together and to be bearers of life, to have children and thus carry out the divine plan of creation. Already in the Book of Genesis, in the story of the creation of man and woman, we find some elements of marriage. "Then God said: 'Let us make man in our image, after our likeness. Let them have dominion over the fish of the sea, the birds of the air, and the cattle, and over all the wild animals and all the creatures that crawl on the ground.' God created man in his image; in the divine image he created him; male and female he created them" (Gn 1:26-27).

Then God commanded them to be fertile and multiply, to fill the earth and subdue it; to have dominion over all living things (cf. Gn 1:28). Unfortunately, because of original sin, this dominion over all creatures was greatly weakened. Nevertheless, the vocation to life and for life is common to every human being, within the framework of the mutual love of husband and wife. Its object is not only the continuation of life but the education and formation of future generations. In this too, husband and wife should reciprocally complement each other.

In the sacrament of matrimony this natural joining of man and woman to each other has been elevated to a higher level, to the level of a sacramental channel of grace. Jesus thus confirms the teaching of the Book of Genesis regarding marriage: "Let no man separate what God has joined" (Mt 19:3-6; cf. Gn 1:27; 2:24). Paul likewise quotes the words of Genesis concerning matrimony and then says: "This is a great foreshadowing; I mean that it refers to Christ and the Church" (Eph 5:31-32).

Christian matrimony has the following characteristics:

1) Unity, meaning that Christian teaching does not permit polygamy, as was prevalent among some people in Old Testament times and is still practiced in some countries. Jesus, instead, insisted: "A man shall leave his father and mother and cling to his wife and the two shall become as one" (Mt 19:5).

2) Indissolubility, which is based on the mutual love between husband and wife, which constitutes a permanent reciprocal bond. Hence, Jesus said: "Everyone who divorces his wife and marries another commits adultery. The man who marries a woman divorced from her husband likewise commits adultery" (Lk 16:18; cf. Mk 10:11-12).

Paul says in this regard: "To those now married, however, I give this command (though it is not mine; it is the Lord's): A wife must not separate from her husband. If she does separate, she must either remain single or become reconciled to him again. Similarly, a husband must not divorce his wife" (1 Cor 7:10-11).

3) Mutual sharing and co-responsibility for education of offspring. The Second Vatican Council has stated: "Marriage and married love are by nature ordered to the procreation and education of children. Indeed, children are the supreme gift of marriage and greatly contribute to the good of the parents themselves" (GS 50; cf. LG 51).

These elements are important safeguards for marriage, home and family. The family is the basic cell of society, and without it society has no future. We must have a strong will to resist the contemporary hedonistic view of life, which fosters sexual immorality, divorce, artificial birth control, abortion, and so many other evils that threaten families today.

The Second Vatican Council has this to say about Christian matrimony: "The intimate union of marriage, as a mutual giving of two persons, and the good of the children demand total fidelity from the spouses and require an unbreakable unity between them" (GS 48).

"In virtue of the sacrament of matrimony by which they signify and share the mystery of the unity and faithful love between Christ and the Church, Christian married couples help one another to attain holiness in their married life and in the rearing of their children. . . . In what might be regarded as the domestic church, the parents by word and example are the first heralds of the faith with regard to their children" (LG 11).

And finally, a word about the celibate life and the life of virginity. To choose God as the highest good and greatest love even in this life is the greatest gift of love that a person can make to God. Some men and women, once they have encountered Christ, have left everything, even their own families, to live for God alone (cf. Lk 14:26; Mk 10:28-31). They form a new family around Christ. "These are my mother and my brothers. Whoever does the will of God is brother and sister and mother to me" (Mk 3:35).

"The Church's holiness is fostered in a special way by the manifold counsels which the Lord proposes to his disciples in the gospel for them to observe. Towering among these counsels is that precious gift of divine grace given to some by the Father to devote themselves more easily to God alone with an undivided heart in virginity or celibacy. This perfect continence for love of the kingdom of heaven has always been held in high esteem by the Church as a sign and stimulus of love, and as a singular source of spiritual fertility in the world" (LG 42).

"By preserving virginity or celibacy for the sake of the kingdom of heaven, priests are consecrated in a new and excellent way to Christ. They more readily cling to him with undivided heart and dedicate themselves more freely in him and through him to the service of God and of men" (PO 16).

Jesus said: "Not everyone can accept this teaching; only those to whom it is given to do so. Some men are incapable of sexual activity from birth; some have been deliberately made so; and some there are who have freely renounced sex for the sake of God's reign. Let him accept this teaching who can" (Mt 19:11-12).

Paul says: "With respect to virgins, I have not received any commandment from the Lord, but I give my opinion as one who is trustworthy, thanks to the Lord's mercy. It is this: In the present time of stress it seems good to me for a person to continue as he is. Are you bound to a wife? Then do not seek your freedom. Are you free of a wife? If so, do not go in search of one. Should you marry, however, you will not be commiting sin. Neither does a virgin commit a sin if she marries. . . . The virgin—indeed, any unmarried woman—is concerned with things of the Lord, in pursuit of holiness in body and spirit. The married woman, on the other hand, has the cares of this world to absorb her and is concerned with pleasing her husband" (1 Cor 7:25-35, passim).

The pure heart is a free heart, free to give, free to love to the point of sacrifice. . . . The pure heart is a heart that serves others, that loves God with an undivided love. The pure heart readily recognizes Christ in the hungry, the lepers, the dying. . . .

The vow of chastity is our response to the invitation of Christ. It is an offering made to God alone, to which we commit ourselves completely in order to live a virginal life in the fervor of charity and in perfect chastity . . . dedicated to Christ and to our neighbor. (Mother Teresa)

One Church or Many?

That all may be one
as you, Father, are in me, and I in you;
I pray that they may be [one] in us,
that the world may believe
that you sent me.
John 17:21

The unity of Christians
is something very important,
because Christians represent
a light for others. Everyone expects of us
that we should live our Christian life
to the full, whether they be Muslim,
Hindu or Christian. The degree to which
we belong to God can be measured
by the way in which we live.
They do not expect us
to condemn, to judge, or to speak
in a way that wounds. . . .
All people are brothers and sisters.
We were created by the same
loving hand of God .
Mother Teresa

The Church is the new people of God, united in Christ by the power of the Holy Spirit. The Church is the sacrament of unity and salvation (cf. LG 12-14). In order to fulfill its providential mission, the Church must first of all be united with God and then with people. This twofold unity is weakened, made difficult, and even broken by sin, which is the source of all division among people. Inevitably it alienates us from God and from neighbor.

Unfortunately, throughout the centuries the Church has been tried and tested by various internal divisions, which are wounds on the Mystical Body of Christ (cf. LG 15; 18-27). Therefore, in order to remain faithful to Christ, the Church must preserve certain essential characteristics:

1) The Church must be firmly established on the word of God, sacred scripture, and tradition (cf. LG 25).

2) The Church should distribute to the faithful the fruits of salvation by administration of the sacraments instituted by Christ and entrusted to the Church (cf. LG 12; 42).

3) The Church must preserve the continuity with the college of the apostles under the primacy of Peter and in union with the modern-day apostles, namely, the bishops and the pope (cf. LG 19-23).

From the earliest days there were difficulties in the Church, and even deviations and erroneous teachings which involved the rejection of some fundamental truths. This led to heresies, meaning an unwillingness to accept all the truths revealed by God, proclaimed by Christ, or taught by the Church, or to interpret some of them erroneously. There have also been internal divisions that affected the local churches. Some of them, as Pope John XXIII said, were "a scandal and a very serious wounding of the Church."

Today there are numerous Christian churches: the Catholic Church, the Orthodox Church, the Anglican Church, and various other Christian denominations. But Jesus Christ is one, and so also should be his Mystical Body the Church (cf. Jn 17:21). Paul wrote: "Make every effort to preserve the unity which has the Spirit as its origin and peace as its binding force. There is but one body and one Spirit, just as there is but one hope given all of you by your call. There is one Lord, one faith, one baptism; one God and Father of all, who is over all, and works through all, and is in all" (Eph 4:3-6).

The Second Vatican Council teaches: "The one Mediator, Christ, established and ever sustains here on earth his holy Church, the community of faith, hope, and charity, as a visible organization through which he communicates truth and grace to all men. . . . This is the sole Church of Christ, which in the Creed we profess to be one, holy, catholic, and apostolic, which our Savior, after his resurrection, entrusted to Peter's pastoral care, commanding him and the other apostles to extend and rule it, and which he raised up for all ages as 'the pillar and mainstay of the truth.' This Church, constituted and organized as a society in the present world, subsists in the Catholic Church, which is governed by the successor of Peter and by the bishops in communion with him" (LG 8).

Now, what should be our attitude toward the other Christian churches? The document of the Second Vatican Council on ecumenism says, among other things: "The Catholic Church accepts them with respect and affection as brothers" (UR 3). The primary purpose of the ecumenical movement is the promotion of unity among separated Christians. This movement is from the Holy Spirit, and in modern times it has had, among others, two outstanding protagonists: Pope John XXIII and the Patriarch Athenagoras I of Istanbul, Turkey.

"Today, in many parts of the world, under the influence of the grace of the Holy Spirit, many efforts are being made in prayer, word, and action to attain that fullness of unity which Jesus Christ desires. This sacred Council exhorts, therefore, all the Catholic faithful to recognize the signs of the times and to take an active and intelligent part in the work of ecumenism" (UR 4). Pope John XXIII founded the Secretariat for Christian Unity in 1960, and the Second Vatican Council published the document *Unitatis Redintegratio* in 1964.

Church unity is a fruit of the grace of God. That is what is sought and being prepared for, and not just a solemn human declaration. To achieve this, we all need an on-going conversion to God and the practice of prayer and fraternal witness "which is the soul of the whole ecumenical movement" (UR 8). In addition to being an ecclesial movement, it also has features that are profoundly social: for example, peace, justice, freedom of peoples, national and international collaboration. The Church of Christ would be much more credible and acceptable in many parts of the world if it could cure the scandal of internal divisions. Pope John XXIII once stated: "The Church is an ancient fountain that gives water to generations of today, as it has done for others in times past. . . . The Church is not a museum; it is a ship that carries salvation to others." In announcing the Second Vatican Council, Pope John XXIII said that it looks not only to the building up of the Christian people but also invites the separated communities to seek unity.

Athenagoras I, the Orthodox Patriarch from Istanbul, Turkey, has said: "The divided Church wounds its Lord, when it should be nothing else but a living chalice in which the divine energy super-abounds for all men. . . . We have made of the Church an organization among so many others. We have spent all our energies in putting it in order, and now we spend energies in trying to make it work. . . . But I believe that the primary, the fundamental condition cannot be anything other than the unity of Christians, who are called to go out in the world together to put themselves at the service of humanity . . . because there is only one Church, the Church of Christ. . . . We talk to one another as brothers and sisters; we pray together. Love is born under the gaze of the Church and transfigures it. The Church and Christianity are beginning to manifest themselves in their common source, which is the gospel and the eucharist."

The Catholic Church has opened its doors and its heart to new meetings with the sister churches, to dialogue with non-Christians and with the whole world (cf. NA 3-4). There is no other way except that of ecumenism and dialogue,F255 because "the man without love has known nothing of God, for God is love" (1 Jn 4:8).

If we are Christians, we ought to resemble Christ. This is my conviction. Gandhi once said that if Christians were truly such, there would be no more Hindus in India. . . . We are all God's children. Some people call him Ishwar; others call him Allah; still others simply call him God; but we should all remember that it is he who has made us for great things. . . . We work with everyone and for everyone and, thanks be to God, we have no difficulty. Our work is ecumenical, because we work with all, without any distinction, in order to approach people among them and to make them know God as love. . . . When love prevails, then we shall have unity of the Church and of the world. (Mother Teresa)